Many and More

Many and More

A Celebration of Love in Later Life

Selected by Jane Mead

TIMKEN PUBLISHERS

Published by Timken Publishers, Inc.
225 Lafayette Street, New York, NY 10012

LIBRARY OF CONGRESS CATALOGUING-IN-PUBLICATION DATA
Many and More : a celebration of love in later life / selected by Jane Mead
p. cm.
ISBN 0-943221-21-8 : $22.00
1. Love in old age—Literary collections. 2. Aged—Literary collections. I. Mead, Jane, 1942– .
PN 6071.L7M35 1994
808.8'0354—dc20 94-5303
CIP

Typeset in Fournier with Medici Script display
Designed and produced by David Bullen
Copyedited by Anna Jardine
Printed in the United States of America

Contents

Foreword

REMARKABLY little has been written from the older lover's point of view. Like the models in our fashion magazines, lovers in books, on the stage, and in the movies have distinctly young faces. Yet love does not depend on firm skin or a slender figure. Certainly experience makes older lovers better lovers. It is one of the benefits of aging that we understand much more of life, and the possibilities of commitment. No longer do we seek in another an answer to ourselves. We require less and may therefore find more. We become more free to love, and if we have listened to ourselves and our past loves, we may love better.

Many and More attempts to fill the gap in the literature of older love. The sources are diverse: poems, short stories, plays, letters, journals, from various lands and times. The earliest text is a poem by Philodemus, who lived in the first century B.C.; the latest is a short story by Ethan Canin published in 1988. Unlike Canin, who was in his twenties when he wrote his story, most of the selected authors writing about love in later life were middle-aged (a relative term, depending on the era) or older. And most of the lovers populating this anthology are themselves close to or beyond—some well beyond—fifty. They speak with honesty, and sometimes humor, about our abiding need for affection, for tenderness, for love, as long as we live.

When we read about these older lovers—or the words they have written—it becomes clear that neither age nor wisdom can spare anyone the pains of love: some of the couples who have been together for a long time are scarred by betrayals, be they petty or large, and some resist love for the inevitable loss that it entails. But those of us who remain open to the possibilities of love in later life will savor its joys and triumphs more strongly than when we were young. For this love is in one important, albeit obvious way, different from love in youth. Time is shorter, mortality looms. Older lovers no longer imagine a whole life with each other. They understand, in Archibald MacLeish's words, that

Ours is the late, last wisdom of the afternoon.
We know that love, like light, grows dearer toward the dark.

Many and More

A Celebration of Love in Later Life

Alice Adams

A Wonderful Woman

Feeling sixteen, although in fact just a few months short of sixty, Felicia Lord checks into the San Francisco hotel at which her lover is to meet her the following day. Felicia is tall and thin, with the intense, somewhat startled look of a survivor—a recent widow, mother of five, a ceramicist who prefers to call herself a potter. A stylish gray-blonde. Mr. Voort, she is told, will be given the room next to hers when he arrives. Smiling to herself, she then follows the ancient wizened bellboy into an antique elevator cage; once inside, as they creakingly ascend, he turns and smiles up at her, as though he knows what she is about. She herself is less sure.

The room to which he leads her is a suite, really: big, shabby-cozy living room, discreetly adjoining bedroom, large old-fashioned bath, on the top floor of this old San Francisco hotel, itself a survivor of the earthquake and fire, in an outlying neighborhood. All in all, she instantly decides, it is the perfect place for meeting Martin, for being with him, in the bright blue dazzling weather, this sudden May.

San Francisco itself, connected as it is with Felicia's own history, has seemed a possibly dangerous choice: the scene of her early, unlikely premarital "romance" with Charles, her now dead husband; then the scene of holiday visits from Connecticut with the children, treat zoo visits and cable-car rides, Chinese restaurants; scene of a passionate ill-advised love affair, and a subsequent abortion—all that also took place in San Francisco, but years ago, in other hotels, other neighborhoods.

Why then, having tipped the grinning bellboy and begun to unpack, silk shirts on hangers, silk tissue-papered nightgowns and underthings in drawers, does she feel such a dizzying lurch of apprehension? It is too intense in its impact to be just a traveler's nerves, jet lag. Felicia is suddenly quite weak; she sits down in an easy chair next to the window to absorb the view, to think sensibly about her situation, or try to. She sees a crazy variety of rooftops: mansard, Victorian curls, old weathered shingles and bright new slate. Blue water, paler sky, green hills. No help.

It is being in love with Martin, she thinks, being "in love," and the newness of Martin Voort. I've never known a farming sailor before, and she smiles, because the words don't describe Martin, really, although he owns some cranberry bogs, near Cape Cod, and he builds boats. Charles was a painter, but he was rich (Martin is not rich) and most of his friends were business people. Martin is entirely new to her.

And at my age, thinks Felicia, and she smiles again, a smile which feels tremulous on her mouth.

"Wonderful" is the word that people generally have used about Felicia. She was wonderful with Charles, whose painting never came to much, although he owned a couple of galleries, who drank a lot. Wonderful to all those kids, who were a little wild, always breaking arms or heads.

Her lover—a Mexican Communist, and like Charles a painter, but a much better painter than Charles—Felipe thought she looked wonderful, with her high-boned face, strong hands and her long, strong voluptuous body. She was wonderful about the abortion, and wonderful too when he went back to his wife.

Felicia was wonderful when Charles died, perfectly controlled and kind to everyone.

Wonderful is not how Felicia sees herself at all; she feels that she has always acted out of simple—or sometimes less simple—necessity.

Once married to Charles, and having seen the lonely, hollow space behind his thin but brilliant surface of good looks, graceful manners, skill at games—it was then impossible to leave him; and he couldn't have stood it. And when the children had terrible coughs, or possible concussions, she took good care of them, sometimes staying up all night, simply because she wanted them well, and soon.

During the unanesthetized abortion, she figured out that you don't scream, because that would surely make the pain much worse, when it is already so bad that it must be happening to someone else, and also because the doctor, a Brazilian chiropractor in the Mission District, is hissing, "Don't make noise." And when your lover defects, saying that he is going back, after all, to his wife in Guadalajara, you don't scream about that either; what good would it do? You go back to your husband, and to the clay pots that you truly love, round and fat or delicately slender.

When your husband dies, as gracefully as he lived, after a too strenuous game of tennis, you take care of everything and everyone, and you behave well, for your own sake as well as for everyone else's.

Then you go to visit an old friend, in Duxbury, and you meet a large wild red-haired, blue-eyed man, a "sailor-farmer," and you fall madly in love, and you agree to meet him for a holiday, in May, in San Francisco, because he has some boats to see there.

She is scared. Sitting there, in the wide sunny window, Felicia trembles, thinking of Martin, the lovely city, themselves, for a long first time. But supposing she isn't "wonderful" anymore? Suppose it all fails, flesh fails, hearts fail, and everything comes crashing down upon their heads, like an avalanche, or an earthquake?

She thinks, I will have to go out for a walk.

Returned from a short tour of the neighborhood, which affords quick beautiful views of the shining bay, and an amazing variety of architecture, Felicia feels herself restored; she is almost her own person again, except for a curious weakness in her legs, and the faintest throb of blood behind one temple, both of which she ascribes to fatigue. She stands there for a moment on the sidewalk, in the sunlight, and then she re-enters the hotel. She is about to walk past the desk when the bellboy, still stationed there, waves something in her direction. A yellow envelope—a telegram.

She thanks him and takes it with her into the elevator, waiting to open it until she is back in her room. It will be from Martin, to welcome her there. Already she knows the character of his gestures: he hates the phone; in fact, so far they have never talked on the telephone, but she has received at least a dozen telegrams from Martin, whose instructions always include: "Deliver, do not phone." After the party at which they met he wired, from Boston to Duxbury: HAVE DINNER WITH ME WILL PICK YOU UP AT SEVEN MARTIN VOORT. Later ones were either jokes or messages of love—or both: from the start they had laughed a lot.

This telegram says: DARLING CRAZY DELAY FEW DAYS LATE ALL LOVE.

The weakness that earlier Felicia had felt in her legs makes them now suddenly buckle; she falls across the bed, and all the blood in both temples pounds as she thinks: I can't stand it, I really can't. This is one thing that is too much for me.

But what do you do if you can't stand something, and you don't scream, after all?

Maybe you just go to bed, as though you were sick?

She undresses, puts on a pretty nightgown and gets into bed, where, like a person with a dangerously high fever, she begins to shake. Her arms crossed over her breast, she clutches both elbows; she presses her ankles together. The tremors gradually subside, and finally, mercifully, she falls asleep, and into dreams. But her sleep is fitful, thin, and from time to time she half wakes from it, never at first sure where she is, nor what year of her life this is.

A long time ago, in the early forties, during Lieutenant (USN) Charles Lord's first leave, he and Felicia Thacher, whom he had invited out to see him, literally danced all night, at all the best hotels in town—as Felicia wondered: Why me? How come Charles picked me for this leave? She had known him since childhood; he was one of her brother's best friends. Had someone else turned him down? She had somewhat the same reactions when he asked her to marry him, over a breakfast glass of champagne, in the Garden Court of the Palace Hotel. Why me? she wondered, and she wondered too at why she was saying yes. She said yes, dreamily, to his urgent eyes, his debonair smile, light voice, in that room full of wartime glamour, uniforms and flowers, partings and poignant brief reunions. Yes, Charles, yes, let's do get married, all right, soon.

A dream of a courtship, and then a dream groom, handsome Charles. And tall, strong-boned, strong-willed Felicia Thacher Lord.

Ironically, since she had so many, Felicia was not especially fond of babies; a highly verbal person, she was nervous with human creatures who couldn't talk, who screamed out their ambiguous demands, who seemed to have no sense and who often smelled terrible. She did not see herself as at all a good mother, knowing how cross and frightened she felt with little children. Good luck (Charles's money) had provided her with helpful nurses all along to relieve her of the children, and the children of her, as she saw it. Further luck made them all turn out all right, on the whole. But thank God she was done with all that. Now she liked all the children very much; she regarded them with great fondness, and some distance.

Her husband, Charles, loved Felicia's pregnancies (well, obviously he did), and all those births, his progeny. He spoke admiringly of how Felicia accomplished all that, her quick deliveries, perfect babies. She began to suspect that Charles had known, in the way that one's unconscious mind knows everything, that this would be the case; he had married her to be the mother of his children.

"I have the perfect situation for a painter, absolutely perfect," Charles once somewhat drunkenly declared. "Big house, perfect studio, money for travel, money to keep the kids away at school. A wonderful kind strong wife. Christ, I even own two galleries. Perfect. I begin to see that the only thing lacking is talent," and he gave a terrible laugh.

How could you leave a man in such despair?

Waking slowly, her head still swollen with sleep, from the tone of the light Felicia guesses that it must be about midafternoon. Eventually she will have to order something to eat, tea or boiled eggs, something sustaining.

Then, with a flash of pain, Martin comes into her mind, and she begins to think.

She simply doesn't know him, that's half the problem, "know" in this instance meaning able to predict the behavior of, really, to trust. Maybe he went to another party and met another available lady, maybe someone rather young, young-fleshed and never sick or tired? (She knows that this could be true, but still it doesn't sound quite right, as little as she knows him.)

But what does FEW DAYS mean to Martin? To some people a week would be a few days. CRAZY DELAY is deliberately ambiguous. Either of those phrases could mean anything at all.

Sinkingly, desparingly, she tells herself that it is sick to have fantasies about the rest of your life that revolve around a man you have only known for a couple of months.

Perfectly possibly he won't come to San Francisco at all, she thinks, and then: I hate this city.

When the bellboy comes in with her supper tray, Felicia realizes for the first time that he is a dwarf; odd that she didn't see that before. His grin now looks malign, contemptuous, even, as though he recognizes her for what she now is: an abandoned woman, of more than a certain age.

As he leaves she shivers, wishing she had brought along a "sensible" robe, practical clothes, instead of all this mocking silk and lace. Looking quickly into the mirror, and then away, she thinks, I look like an old circus monkey.

She sleeps through the night. One day gone, out of whatever "few days" are.

When she calls to order breakfast the next morning, the manager (manageress: a woman with a strong, harsh midwestern accent) suggests firmly that a doctor should be called. She knows of one.

Refusing that suggestion, as firmly, politely as she can, Felicia knows that she reacted to hostility rather than to concern. The manageress is afraid that Felicia will get really sick and die; what a mess to have on their hands, an unknown dead old woman.

But Felicia too is a little afraid.

Come to think of it, Felicia says to herself, half waking at what must be the middle of the afternoon, I once spent some time in another San Francisco hotel, waiting for Felipe, in another part of town. After the abortion.

She and Felipe met when he had a show at one of Charles's galleries; they had, at first tipsily, fallen into bed, in Felipe's motel (Charles had "gone to sleep") after the first reception; then soberly, both passionately serious, they fell in love. Felipe's paintings were touring the country, Felipe with them, and from time to time, in various cities, Felicia followed him. Her excuse to Charles was a survey of possible markets for her pots, and visits to other potters, which, conscientiously, she also accomplished.

Felipe was as macho as he was radical, and he loved her in his own macho way, violently, with all his dangerous strength. She must leave Charles, Charles must never touch her again, he said. (Well,

Charles drank so much that that was hardly an issue.) She must come with him to Paris, to a new life. All her children were by then either grown or off in schools—why not?

When they learned that she was pregnant he desperately wanted their child, he said, but agreed that a child was not possible for them. And he remembered the Brazilian chiropractor that he had heard about, from relatives in San Francisco.

The doctor seemingly did a good job, for Felicia suffered no later ill effects. Felipe was kind and tender with her; he said that her courage had moved him terribly. Felicia felt that her courage, if you wanted to call it that, had somewhat unnerved him; he was a little afraid of her now.

However, they celebrated being together in San Francisco, where Felipe had not been before. He loved the beautiful city, and they toasted each other, and their mutual passion, with Mexican beer or red wine, in their Lombard Street motel. Then one afternoon Felipe went off alone to visit a family of his relatives, in San Jose, and Felicia waited for him. He returned to her very late, and in tears: a grown man, broad-backed, terrifically strong, with springing thick black hair and powerful arms, crying out to her, "I cannot—I cannot go on with you, with our life. They have told me of my wife, all day she cries, and at night she screams and wakes the children. I must go to her."

Well, of course you must, said Felicia, in effect. If she's screaming that's where you belong. And she thought, Well, so much for my Latin love affair.

And she went home.

And now she thinks, Martin at least will not come to me in tears.

Martin Voort. At the end of her week in Duxbury, her visit to the old school friend, Martin, whom in one way or another she had seen every day, asked her to marry him, as soon as possible. "Oh, I know we're both over the hill," he said, and then exploded in a laugh, as she did too. "But suppose we're freaks who live to be a hundred? We might as well have a little fun on the way. I like you a lot. I want to be with you."

Felicia laughed again. She was secretly pleased that he hadn't said she was wonderful, but she thought he was a little crazy.

He followed her home with telegrams: WHEN OH WHEN WILL YOU MARRY ME and ARRIVING IN YOUR TOWN THIS FRIDAY PREPARE.

And now, suppose she never sees him again? For the first time in many months (actually, since Charles died) Felicia begins to cry, at the possible loss of such a rare, eccentric and infinitely valuable man.

But in the midst of her sorrow at that terrible possibility, the permanent lack of Martin—who could be very sick, could have had a stroke: at his age, their age, that is entirely possible—though grieving, Felicia realizes that she can stand it, after all, as she has stood other losses, other sorrows in her life. She can live without Martin.

She realizes too that she herself has just been genuinely ill, somewhat frighteningly so; what she had was a real fever, from whatever cause. Perhaps she should have seen a doctor.

However, the very thought of a doctor, a doctor's office, is enough to make her well, she dislikes them so; all those years of children, children's illnesses and accidents, made her terribly tired of medical treatment. Instead she will get dressed and go out for dinner, by herself.

And that is what she does. In her best clothes she takes a cab to what has always been her favorite San Francisco restaurant, Sam's. It is quite early, the place uncrowded. Felicia is given a pleasant side table, and the venerable waiters are kind to her. The seafood is marvelous. Felicia drinks a half-bottle of wine with her dinner and she thinks: Oh, so this is what it will be like. Well, it's really not so bad.

Returned to the hotel, however, once inside her room she experiences an acute pang of disappointment, and she understands that she had half-consciously expected Martin to be there; Martin was to be her reward for realizing that she could live without him, for being "sensible," for bravely going out to dinner by herself.

She goes quickly to bed, feeling weak and childish, and approving neither her weakness nor her childishness, not at all.

Sometime in the middle of the night she awakes from a sound sleep, and from a vivid dream; someone, a man, has knocked on the door of her room, this room. She answers, and he comes in and they embrace, and she is wildly glad to see him. But who is he? She can't tell: Is it her husband, Charles, or one of her sons? Felipe? Is it Martin? It could even be a man she doesn't know. But fully awake, as she considers the dream she is saddened by it, and it is quite a while before she sleeps again.

The next morning, though, she is all right: refreshed, herself again. Even in the mirror, her face is all right. I look like what I am, she thinks: a strong healthy older woman. She dresses and goes downstairs to breakfast, beginning to plan her day. Both the bellboy and the manager smile in a relieved way as she passes the desk, and she smiles back, amiably.

She will see as much of San Francisco as possible today, and arrange to leave tomorrow. Why wait around? This morning she will take a cab to Union Square, and walk from there along Grant Avenue, Chinatown, to North Beach, where she will have lunch. Then back to the hotel for a nap, then a walk, and dinner out—maybe Sam's again.

She follows the plan, or most of it. On Union Square, she goes into a couple of stores, where she looks at some crazily overpriced clothes, and buys one beautiful gauzy Indian scarf, for a daughter's coming birthday. Then down to Grant Avenue, to walk among the smells of Chinese food, the incense, on to North Beach, to a small Italian counter restaurant, where she has linguine with clam sauce, and a glass of red wine.

In the cab, going back to the hotel, she knows that she is too tired, has "overdone," but it was worth it. She has enjoyed the city, after all.

An hour or so later, from a deep, deep sleep she is awakened by a knocking on her door, just as in her dream, the night before.

Groggily she calls out, "Who is it?" She is not even sure that the sound has been real; so easily this could be another dream.

A man's impatient, irritated voice answers, "It's *me*, of course."

Me? She is still half asleep; she doesn't know who he is. However, his tone has made her obedient, and she gets out of bed, pulling her robe about her, and she goes to the door. And there is a tall, red-haired man, with bright blue eyes, whom of course she knows, was expecting—who embraces her violently. "Ah, Martin," she breathes, when she can.

It is Martin, and she is awake.

The only unfamiliar thing about his face, she notes, when she can see him, is that a tooth is missing from his smile; there is a small gap that he covers with his hand as soon as she has noticed. And he says, "It broke right off! Right off a bridge. And my dentist said I'd have to wait a week. How could I send you a telegram about a goddamn dentist? Anyway, I couldn't wait a week to see you."

They laugh (although there are tears somewhere near Felicia's eyes), and then they embrace again.

And at last they are sitting down on the easy chairs near the window, next to the view, and they are quietly talking together, making plans for the rest of that day and night.

Paul the Silentiary

Poem

CHOICER than all
flush of youth
is your wrinkled prime,
            Philinna:
my hands long for
the mellow fruit,
heavy, that fills
them full—not
for a girl's breasts,
unripe. Know,

love, your autumnal
wealth outdoes
another's spring,
                    your frost
her summer's heat.

Bernard Slade

ACT II, SCENES 2 AND 3

from Same Time, Next Year:

A Comedy in Two Acts

ACT TWO, *Scene 2*

THE TIME: *A day in February, 1970.*

THE PLACE: *A bed-sitting room in the guest cottage of a Spanish-style inn near Mendocino, north of San Francisco. It is a cozy, comfortable room, large enough to contain a double bed, dressing table, chintz-covered sofa, baby grand piano, wood-burning fireplace and ottoman. There are two leaded-pane glass windows, a closet, a door leading to the bathroom and another door which opens onto the patio-entrance to the cottage. The room's aura of permanence is not an illusion. The decor has been the same for the past twenty-five years and will not change for the next twenty-five.*

AT RISE: *Doris and George are sitting up in bed. She is doing a crossword puzzle. He is reading the sports section of a newspaper. After a few moments, they put down their papers and look at each other.*

DORIS: It's amazing how good it can be after twenty years, isn't it?

GEORGE: Honey, if you add up all the times we've actually made it together, we're still on our honeymoon.

DORIS: Did I tell you I'm a grandmother?

GEORGE: No, but I think you picked a weird time to announce it. Anyway, you're the youngest-looking grandmother I've ever had a peak experience with.

DORIS: *(She crosses to dressing table.)* My mother thanks you, my father thanks you, my hairdresser thanks you and my plastic surgeon thanks you. *(She sits at dresser, peers into mirror, starts to brush hair and apply makeup.)* When Harry says, "You're not the girl I married," he doesn't know how right he is.

GEORGE: Didn't Harry like your old nose?

DORIS: Harry thinks this is my old nose.

GEORGE: He never noticed?

DORIS: Pathetic, isn't it? A new dress I could understand—but a whole nose?

GEORGE: Well . . . *(He gets blue jeans and puts them on.)* to be totally honest I really can't see much of a difference either.

DORIS: I don't care. It's different from my side. Makes me feel more attractive.

GEORGE: Why do you need a validation of your attractiveness?

DORIS: A woman starts feeling a little insecure when she gets to be forty-four.

GEORGE: Forty-five.

DORIS: See what I mean? Anyway, that's this year's bad story about Harry. Got one about Helen?

GEORGE: There was a loud party next door. Helen couldn't sleep and she didn't want to take a sleeping pill because she had to get up at six the next morning. So she stuffed two pills in her ears. During the night they melted. The next morning as the doctor was digging the stuff out of her ears he said, "You know these can be taken orally." Helen just laughed. She doesn't care.

DORIS: If that's the worst story you can tell about your wife you must be a very happy man.

GEORGE: Well, let's say I've discovered I have the potential for happiness. *(The phone rings.)*

DORIS: Hello. Oh hi, Liz. No, it's sixty—not sixteen guests—that's right, a brunch. We've catered a couple of parties for her before—no problem. She sets up tables around the pool and there's room for the buffet on the patio. Right. Oh, Liz, did Harry call? Okay, I'll be at this number. *(She hangs up.)* Sorry, busy weekend. I had to leave a number.

GEORGE: Does Harry know you're here?

DORIS: No, Harry still thinks I go on retreat. Don't worry. *(She continues to make up during the following.)*

GEORGE: I'm not worried.

DORIS: Then why are you frowning?

GEORGE: Because I'm getting bad vibes again.

DORIS: Again?

GEORGE: When you walked in I sensed your high tension level. Then after we made love I noticed a certain anxiety reduction, but now I'm getting a definite negative feedback.

DORIS: When did you go into analysis?

GEORGE: How did you know I was in analysis?

DORIS: Just a wild guess. What made you start?

GEORGE: My value system changed. One day I took a look at my $150,000 house, the three cars in the garage, the swimming pool, and the gardeners. I asked myself did I really want the whole status trip? So—I decided to try and find out what I did want and who I was.

(Doris has gotten lounging pajamas from suitcase and exited into bathroom.)

DORIS: *(Offstage.)* And you went from analysis to Esalen to Gestalt to Transactional to encounter groups to Nirvana.

GEORGE: Doris, just because some people are trying to widen their emotional horizons doesn't make the experience any less valid. I've learned a lot.

DORIS: *(Offstage.)* I've noticed. For one thing you learned to talk as if you're reasoning with someone about to jump off a high ledge. *(She enters and crosses to George for help with her zipper.)*

GEORGE: Sometimes to compensate for my former emotionalism I tend to overcompensate and tend to lose some of my spontaneity. I'm working on that.

DORIS: I'm glad to hear it. What else have you learned?

GEORGE: I've learned that behind the walls I've built around myself I can be a very warm, caring, loving human being.

DORIS: I could have told you that twenty years ago. Tell me, how's Helen reacting to your "voyage of self-discovery"?

GEORGE: At first she tended to overreact.

DORIS: In what way?

GEORGE: She threw a grapefruit at me in the A&P. It was natural that we'd have to work through some interpersonal conflicts, but now it's cool. She's into pottery. *(George sits at piano and starts to play.)*

DORIS: What do you do for a living?

GEORGE: We live very simply, Doris. We don't need much. What bread we do need I can provide by simple, honest labor.

DORIS: Like what?

GEORGE: I play cocktail piano in a singles bar in the valley. *(The phone rings again. Before answering, Doris looks at George. He stops playing.)*

DORIS: Hello. Yes, Liz? No way. Tell him that's our final offer—I don't care how good a location it is—That's bull, Liz, he needs us more than we need him. If he doesn't like it he can shove it, but don't worry—he won't. Anything else? You know where to reach me. *(She hangs up.)* I'm buying another store.

GEORGE: *(He starts playing again.)* Why?

DORIS: Money.

GEORGE: Is that why you went into business? To make money?

DORIS: No, I wanted power too. And it finally got through my thick skull that attending C.R. groups with ten other frustrated housewives wasn't going to change anything.

GEORGE: C.R. groups?

DORIS: Consciousness-raising. I take it you are for women's liberation?

GEORGE: Hey, I'm for any kind of liberation.

DORIS: That's a cop-out and you know it. Women have always been exploited by men.

GEORGE: *(He stops playing.)* We've all been shafted, Doris, and by the same things. Look, let me lay this on you. I go to a woman doctor. The first time she gave me a rectal examination she said, "Am I hurting you or are you tense?" I said, "I'm tense." She said, "Are you tense because I'm a woman?" and I said, "No, I get tense when anybody does that to me." You see what I mean?

DORIS: I don't know, but I do know that the only time a woman is taken seriously in this country is when she has the money to back up her mouth.

GEORGE: I think it's great to have a hobby.

DORIS: Hobby? We grossed over half a million the first year.

GEORGE: Honey, don't misunderstand. If that's what you want I'm very happy for you. It's just that I'm not into the money thing anymore.

DORIS: Do you ever get the feeling we're drifting apart?

GEORGE: No. In many ways I've never felt closer to you.

DORIS: I don't know, sometimes I think our lives are getting—out of sync.

GEORGE: We all realize our potential in different ways at different times. As long as what you're doing gives you a sense of fulfillment, that's what's important.

DORIS: Well, I'm working on it.

GEORGE: And do you have everything you want?

DORIS: With one minor exception. Somewhere along the way I seem to have lost my husband.

GEORGE: Lost him?

DORIS: Well, I don't know if I've lost him or simply misplaced him. He left home four days ago and I haven't heard from him since.

GEORGE: How do you feel about that?

DORIS: George, do me a favor—stop talking as though you're leading a human potential group. It really pisses me off.

GEORGE: That's cool.

DORIS: What's cool?

GEORGE: For you to transfer your feelings of aggression and hostility from Harry to me. As long as you know that's what you're doing.

DORIS: You know something, George? You're beginning to get on my nerves.

GEORGE: That's cool, too.

DORIS: Jesus.

GEORGE: I mean it. At least it's honest. Total honesty is the key to everything.

DORIS: Are you being totally honest with Helen?

GEORGE: I'm trying.

DORIS: Have you told her about us?

GEORGE: No—but I could. Really, I think that today she's mature enough to handle it.

DORIS: George, you're full of shit.

GEORGE: I can buy that—if you're really being honest.

DORIS: Believe me, I'm being honest!

GEORGE: But what about that garbage about "I don't know if I lost him or simply misplaced him." I mean, what sort of crap is that?

DORIS: Okay, you have a point.

GEORGE: So how do you feel about all this?

DORIS: You're doing it again, George.

GEORGE: I know I'm doing it. How do you feel about this?

DORIS: Okay, I think . . .

GEORGE: No, don't tell me how you think. Tell me how you feel.

DORIS: Like I've been kicked in the stomach.

GEORGE: That's good. What else?

DORIS: Angry, hurt, betrayed and—okay, a little guilty. But you know something? I *resent* the fact that he's making me feel guilty.

GEORGE: How do you feel resentment?

DORIS: Look, I didn't marry Harry because he had a good head for business! Okay, it so happens that I discovered I did. Or maybe I was just lucky—I don't know. The point is, I don't love Harry any less because he's a failure as a provider. Why should he love me any less because I'm a success? At least I think that's how I feel.

GEORGE: You're not sure?

DORIS: It varies between Joan of Arc and Betty Crocker.

GEORGE: We're all going through transitional periods.

DORIS: What do I do about now?

GEORGE: Have you told him you still love him?

DORIS: Love him? Why does he think I've been hanging around for twenty-seven years?

GEORGE: I just mean that right now his masculinity is being threatened and he probably needs some validation of his worth as a man.

DORIS: And how do I do that? That's some trick.

GEORGE: Total honesty, Doris. Is it so hard for you to tell him that you understand how he feels?

DORIS: Right now—it is, yes.

GEORGE: You want him back?

DORIS: I don't know. Ask me tomorrow and I'll probably give you a different answer.

GEORGE: Why?

DORIS: Tomorrow I won't have you.

GEORGE: I'm always with you in spirit.

DORIS: Thanks a lot. It's kind of hard to put your cold feet on someone's spirit, isn't it? Especially when they're four hundred miles away.

GEORGE: Is that a proposal, Doris?

DORIS: Why, you interested?

GEORGE: Are you?

DORIS: I always thought we'd make a nice couple.

GEORGE: You didn't answer the question.

DORIS: I was the one who proposed. But don't worry, I was only three-quarters serious.

GEORGE: Well, when you are completely serious why don't you ask me again.

DORIS: I bet you say that to all the girls.

GEORGE: No.

DORIS: Thanks.

GEORGE: Stop feeling so insecure.

DORIS: About what?

GEORGE: You're as feminine as you've always been.

DORIS: Gloria Steinem is going to hate me for this, but I sure am glad you said that. I guess I'm not as emancipated as I thought, huh?

GEORGE: None of us are.

DORIS: You hungry?

GEORGE: Yes.

DORIS: Well, you're in luck because tonight our dinner is being catered by the chicest, most expensive French delicatessen in San Francisco.

GEORGE: How'd we swing that?

DORIS: The owner has a thing for you. *(She moves toward the front door.)* It's in the trunk of my car.

GEORGE: You want help?

DORIS: Yes. Set the table, light the candles, and when I come back make me laugh.

GEORGE: I'll try.

DORIS: Don't worry. If you can't make me laugh just hold my hand. *(She exits. After a few moments, the phone rings. George hesitates for a moment before answering.)*

GEORGE: Hello. No, she's not here right now. Who's calling, please? Harry!—Hold on a moment, please. *(He hesitates for a few minutes.)* Hello—Harry, we're two adult, mature human beings and

I've decided to be totally honest with you. . . . No, Doris is not here right now but I'd like to talk to you. . . . I know you and Doris have been having difficulties lately and . . . We're very close friends. I've known Doris for twenty years and through her I feel as if I know you. . . . Well, we've been meeting this same weekend for twenty years— The retreat? Well, we can get into that later, but first I want you to know something. She loves you, Harry. . . . —she really loves you—I just know, Harry. Look, maybe if I told you a story she just told me this morning it would help you understand. A few months ago Doris was supposed to act as a den mother for your ten-year-old daughter and her Indian Guide group. Well, she got hung up at the store and was two hours late getting home. When she walked into the house she looked into the living room, and do you know what she saw? A rather overweight, balding, middle-aged man with a feather on his head sitting cross-legged on the floor very gravely and gently telling a circle of totally absorbed little girls what it was like to be in a World War II Japanese prison camp. She turned around, walked out, and sat in her car and thanked God for being married to a man like you. . . . Are you still there, Harry? Well, sometimes married people get into an emotional straitjacket and find it difficult to express how they truly feel about each other. Total honesty is the key. Yes, I've known Doris for twenty years, and I'm not ashamed to admit that it's been one of the most intimate, satisfying experiences of my life. . . . My name? My name is Father Michael O'Herlihy.

CURTAIN

END OF ACT TWO, *scene 2*

ACT TWO, *Scene 3*

THE TIME: *A day in February, 1975.*

THE PLACE: *The same.*

AT RISE: *Doris enters from the bathroom with a large bouquet of red roses which she places on the piano. She then crosses to the dressing table with her purse and books. She views her figure in the mirror trying to hold it in youthful posture. She is about to give up when the door opens and George enters. They embrace affectionately.*

GEORGE: You feel so good.

DORIS: So do you. But you *look* tired. You okay?

GEORGE: I've looked this way for years. You just haven't noticed. Anyway, I feel better now I'm here. This room's always had an effect on me.

DORIS: It never changes, does it?

GEORGE: About the only thing that doesn't.

DORIS: I find that comforting.

GEORGE: Even old Chalmers is the same. He must be seventy-five by now. He must have been about the same age then we are now.

DORIS: That I don't find so comforting.

GEORGE: We were very young.

DORIS: Have we changed much?

GEORGE: Of course. I grew up with you. Remember the dumb lies I used to tell?

DORIS: I miss them.

GEORGE: I don't. It was no fun being that insecure.

DORIS: And what about me? Have I grown up too?

GEORGE: I have the feeling you were already grown up when I met you. Tell me something.

DORIS: Anything.

GEORGE: Why is it that every time I look at you I want to put my hands all over you?

DORIS: That's another thing that hasn't changed. You were always a sex maniac.

GEORGE: Let's see if I can get a fire going. *(He crosses to the fireplace.)* You know, I figured out with the cost of firewood it's cheaper to buy furniture, break it up, and burn it.

DORIS: Things that tight?

GEORGE: No, I'm okay. I've been doing some teaching at UCLA.

DORIS: Music?

GEORGE: Accounting. The way things keep changing, figures are still the only things that don't lie. *(She moves to pour two cups of coffee from a coffeepot on the coffee table.)* Doris, why'd you sell your business?

DORIS: How did you know that?

GEORGE: I'll tell you later. What made you do it?

DORIS: I was bought out by a chain. It was the right offer at the right time.

GEORGE: You don't miss the action?

DORIS: Not yet. I guess I'm still enjoying being one of the idle rich.

GEORGE: But what do you do with yourself?

DORIS: Oh, read, watch TV, play a little golf, visit my grandchildren—you know, all the jet-set stuff.

GEORGE: I thought you loved working.

DORIS: Well, there was another factor. Harry had a heart attack. It turned out to be a mild one, but he needed me at the time. Anyway, it's not as if I'm in permanent retirement. There's a local election coming up in a few months and I've been approached to run.

GEORGE: On what ticket?

DORIS: Independent.

GEORGE: Figures. Harry's okay now?

DORIS: Runs four miles a day and has a body like Mark Spitz. Unfortunately, he still has a face like Ernest Borgnine's. You want to hear a nice story about him?

GEORGE: Sure.

DORIS: When they were wheeling him out of intensive care he looked up at the doctor and said, "Doc, give it to me straight. After I get out of here will I be able to play the piano?" The doctor said, "Of course." And Harry said, "Funny, I couldn't when I came in." The thing is Harry never makes jokes, but he saw how panicky I was and he wanted to make me feel better.

GEORGE: How are you and Harry . . . emotionally?

DORIS: Comfortable.

GEORGE: Comfortable?

DORIS: Oh, it's not such a bad state. The word's been given a bad reputation by the young. *(She looks around.)* Where's your luggage? Still in the car?

GEORGE: I didn't bring any. I can't stay, Doris.

DORIS: Why?

GEORGE: Look, I have so much to say and a short time to say it, so I'd better start. First of all, Helen's known about us for ten years.

DORIS: When did you find that out?

GEORGE: Two months ago.

DORIS: She never confronted you with it before?

GEORGE: No.

DORIS: What made her tell you now?

GEORGE: She didn't. We have a very close friend, Connie—have I mentioned her before? Connie told me. Ten years and she never even hinted that she knew. That may be the nicest story I've ever told about her.

DORIS: Your wife's an amazing woman.

GEORGE: She passed away, Doris. I lost her six months ago. It was all—very fast. I'm sorry to blurt it out like that. I just couldn't think of a—a graceful way to tell you. You okay, honey?

DORIS: It's so strange. I never met Helen and I feel as if I've just lost my best friend. It's—crazy. Are the kids okay?

GEORGE: They'll survive. I don't think I could have gotten through the whole thing without them.

DORIS: I just wish you'd tried to reach me.

GEORGE: I did. That's when I'd found you'd sold the stores. I called and they gave me your home number. I let the phone ring four times, then I hung up. But it made me feel better knowing you were there if I needed you.

DORIS: I wish you'd spoken to me.

GEORGE: I didn't want to intrude. I didn't feel I had the right.

DORIS: My God, that's terrible. We should have been together.

GEORGE: I've been thinking about us a lot lately. Everything we've been through together. The things we've shared. The times we've helped each other. Did you know we've made love a hundred and thirteen times? I figured it out on my Bomar calculator. *(He is fixing fresh cups of coffee.)* It's a wonderful thing to know someone that well. You know, there is nothing about you I don't know. It's two sugars, right?

DORIS: No, one.

GEORGE: So I don't know everything about you. I don't know who your favorite movie stars are and I couldn't remember the name of your favorite perfume. I wracked my brain but I couldn't remember.

DORIS: That's funny. It's My Sin.

GEORGE: But I do know that in twenty-four years I've never been out of love with you. I find that incredible. So what do you say, Doris, you want to get married?

DORIS: *(Lightly.)* Married? We shouldn't even be doing this.

GEORGE: I'm serious.

DORIS: *(Looking at him.)* You really are, aren't you?

GEORGE: What did you think I was—just another summer romance? A simple "yes" will do.

DORIS: There's no such thing.

GEORGE: What is it?

DORIS: I was just thinking of how many times I've dreamed of you asking me this. It's pulled me through a lot of bad times. I want to thank you for that.

GEORGE: What did you say to me all those times?

DORIS: I always said "yes."

GEORGE: And you're hesitating now? *(Pause.)* Do you realize I'm giving you the opportunity to marry a man who has known you for twenty-four years and cannot walk by you without wanting to grab your ass?

DORIS: You always were a sweet talker.

GEORGE: That's because if I told you how I really felt about you, it would probably sound like a medley of clichés from popular songs. Will you marry me?

DORIS: *(Pause.)* I can't.

GEORGE: Why not?

DORIS: I'm already married.

GEORGE: You feel you have to stay because he needs you?

DORIS: No it's a lot of things—affection, respect, a sense of continuity. We share all the same memories. It's—comfortable. Maybe that's what marriage is all about in the end—I don't know.

GEORGE: Will you tell me why I had to be so stupid five years ago to help you get back together? I mean, why was I so damned generous?

DORIS: Because you felt the same way about Helen then as I do about Harry now. And if I hadn't gone back to Harry, you might have been stuck with me permanently, and you were terrified.

GEORGE: You could always see through me, couldn't you?

DORIS: That's okay. I always loved what I saw.

GEORGE: Well, I want you now.

DORIS: You can still have me once a year. Same time, same place.

GEORGE: Doris, I need a wife. I'm just not the kind of man who can live alone. I want you to marry me, but when I came here I—I knew there was a chance you'd say "no." What I'm trying to say is—without you, I'll probably end up with Connie. She knows—all about you. The point is, she's not the sort of woman who would accept the situation. I suppose what I'm saying is that we'll probably never see each other again. You're trembling.

DORIS: The thought of never seeing you again absolutely terrifies me.

GEORGE: Doris, for God's sake—marry me!

DORIS: I can't. *(Pause.)*

GEORGE: I wish I could think of something that would break your heart, make you burst into tears and come away with me.

DORIS: You know us Italians. We never cry.

GEORGE: *(Going for his coat.)* I've got to catch a plane. What time is it? *(She holds out her wrist.)* Five fifty-five?

DORIS: No, I keep my watch three hours and twenty-five minutes fast.

GEORGE: How long have you been doing that?

DORIS: Twenty-odd years.

GEORGE: Why would anyone do a thing like that?

DORIS: Personal idiosyncrasy.

GEORGE: Who were your favorite movie stars?

DORIS: Lon McAllister, Cary Grant, Marlon Brando, and Laurence Olivier.

GEORGE: You've come such a long way.

DORIS: We both have.

GEORGE: Always keep your watch three hours and twenty-five minutes fast, huh. *(A beat.)* I can't believe this is happening to us. *(He exits quickly, shutting the door behind him. Doris stands for a moment trying to absorb the shock of his departure. Doris finally can contain her tears no longer. She throws herself facedown on the bed. The door crashes open and George bursts into the room with his suitcase.)* Okay, I'm back, goddammit!

DORIS: What about Connie?

GEORGE: Connie's eighty-nine years old! *(Doris laughs.)* Look, I wanted you to marry me, and I figured if you thought someone else wanted me I might stand a better chance . . . I was desperate, okay? Look, for once in my life I wanted a happy ending. Listen, I don't want to talk about it anymore. I'm back and I'm going to keep coming back every year until our bones are too brittle to risk contact. *(Doris and George embrace as—)*

THE CURTAIN FALLS

Pablo Neruda

Sonnet

I thought I was dying, I felt the cold up close
and knew that from all my life I left only you behind:
my earthly day and night were your mouth,
your skin the republic my kisses founded.

In that instant the books stopped,
and friendship, treasures restlessly amassed,
the transparent house that you and I built:
everything dropped away, except your eyes.

Because while life harasses us, love is
only a wave taller than the other waves:
but oh, when death comes knocking at the gate,

there is only your glance against so much emptiness,
only your light against extinction,
only your love to shut out the shadows.

William Shakespeare

Sonnet

THAT time of year thou mayst in me behold
When yellow leaves, or none, or few, do hang
Upon those boughs which shake against the cold,
Bare ruined choirs, where late the sweet birds sang.
In me thou seest the twilight of such day
As after sunset fadeth in the west,
Which by and by black night doth take away,
Death's second self, that seals up all the rest.
In me thou seest the glowing of such fire
That on the ashes of his youth doth lie,

As the deathbed whereon it must expire,
Consumed with that which it was nourished by.
This thou perceiv'st, which makes thy love more strong,
To love that well which thou must leave ere long.

Ethan Canin

We Are Nighttime Travelers

Where are we going? Where, I might write, is this path leading us? Francine is asleep and I am standing downstairs in the kitchen with the door closed and the light on and a stack of mostly blank paper on the counter in front of me. My dentures are in a glass by the sink. I clean them with a tablet that bubbles in the water, and although they were clean already I just cleaned them again because the bubbles are agreeable and I thought their effervescence might excite me to action. By action, I mean I thought they might excite me to write. But words fail me.

This is a love story. However, its roots are tangled and involve a good bit of my life, and when I recall my life my mood turns sour and I am reminded that no man makes truly proper use of his time. We are blind and small-minded. We are dumb as snails and as frightened, full of vanity and misinformed about the importance of things. I'm an average man, without great deeds except maybe one, and that has been to love my wife.

I have been more or less faithful to Francine since I married her. There has been one transgression—leaning up against a closet wall with a red-haired purchasing agent at a sales meeting once in Minneapolis twenty years ago; but she was buying auto upholstery and I was selling it and in the eyes of judgment this may bear a key weight. Since then, though, I have ambled on this narrow path of life bound to one woman. This is a triumph and a regret. In our current state of affairs it is a regret because in life a man is either on the uphill or the downhill, and if he isn't procreating he is on the downhill. It is a steep downhill indeed. These days I am tumbling, falling headlong among the scrub oaks and boulders, tearing my knees and abrading all the bony parts of the body. I have given myself to gravity.

Francine and I are married now forty-six years, and I would be a bamboozler to say that I have loved her for any more than half of these. Let us say that for the last year I haven't; let us say this for the last ten, even. Time has made torments of our small differences and tolerance of our passions. This is our state of affairs. Now I stand by myself in our kitchen in the middle of the night; now I lead a secret life. We wake at different hours now, sleep in different corners of the bed. We like different foods and different music, keep our clothing in different drawers, and if it can be said that either of us has aspirations, I believe that they are to a different bliss. Also, she is healthy and I am ill. And as for conversation—that feast of reason, that flow of the soul—our house is silent as the bone yard.

Last week we did talk. "Frank," she said one evening at the table, "there is something I must tell you."

The New York game was on the radio, snow was falling outside, and the pot of tea she had brewed was steaming on the table between us. Her medicine and my medicine were in little paper cups at our places.

"Frank," she said, jiggling her cup, "what I must tell you is that someone was around the house last night."

I tilted my pills onto my hand. "Around the house?"

"Someone was at the window."

On my palm the pills were white, blue, beige, pink: Lasix, Diabinese, Slow-K, Lopressor. "What do you mean?"

She rolled her pills onto the tablecloth and fidgeted with them, made them into a line, then into a circle, then into a line again. I don't know her medicine so well. She's healthy, except for little things. "I mean," she said, "there was someone in the yard last night."

"How do you know?"

"Frank, will you really, please?"

"I'm asking how you know."

"I heard him," she said. She looked down. "I was sitting in the front room and I heard him outside the window."

"You heard him?"

"Yes."

"The front window?"

She got up and went to the sink. This is a trick of hers. At that distance I can't see her face.

"The front window is ten feet off the ground," I said.

"What I know is that there was a man out there last night, right outside the glass." She walked out of the kitchen.

"Let's check," I called after her. I walked into the living room, and when I got there she was looking out the window.

"What is it?"

She was peering out at an angle. All I could see was snow, blue-white.

"Footprints," she said.

I BUILT the house we live in with my two hands. That was forty-nine years ago, when, in my foolishness and crude want of learning, everything I didn't know seemed like a promise. I learned to build a house and then I built one. There are copper fixtures on the pipes, sanded edges on the struts and queen posts. Now, a half-century later, the floors are flat as a billiard table but the man who laid them needs two hands to pick up a woodscrew. This is the diabetes. My feet are gone also. I look down at them and see two black shapes when I walk, things I can't feel. Black clubs. No connection with the ground. If I didn't look, I could go to sleep with my shoes on.

Life takes its toll, and soon the body gives up completely. But it gives up the parts first. This sugar in the blood: God says to me: "Frank Manlius—codger, man of prevarication and half-truth—I shall take your life from you, as from all men. But first—" But first! Clouds in the eyeball, a heart that makes noise, feet cold as uncooked roast. And Francine, beauty that she was—now I see not much more than the dark line of her brow and the intersections of her body: mouth and nose, neck and shoulders. Her smells have changed over the years so that I don't know what's her own anymore and what's powder.

We have two children, but they're gone now too, with children of their own. We have a house, some furniture, small savings to speak of. How Francine spends her day I don't know. This is the sad truth, my confession. I am gone past nightfall. She wakes early with me and is awake when I return, but beyond this I know almost nothing of her life.

I myself spend my days at the aquarium. I've told Francine something else, of course, that I'm part of a volunteer service of retired men, that we spend our days setting young businesses afoot: "Immigrants," I told her early on, "newcomers to the land." I said it was difficult work. In the evenings I could invent stories, but I don't, and Francine doesn't ask.

I am home by nine or ten. Ticket stubs from the aquarium fill my coat pocket. Most of the day I watch the big sea animals—porpoises, sharks, a manatee—turn their saltwater loops. I come late morning and move a chair up close. They are waiting to eat then. Their bodies skim the cool glass, full of strange magnifications. I think, if it is possible, that they are beginning to know me: this man—hunched at the shoulder, cataractic of eye, breathing through water himself—this man who sits and watches. I do not pity them. At lunchtime I buy coffee and sit in one of the hotel lobbies or in the cafeteria next door, and I read poems. Browning, Whitman, Eliot. This is my secret. It is night when I return home. Francine is at the table, four feet across from my seat, the width of two dropleaves. Our medicine is in cups. There have been three Presidents since I held her in my arms.

THE CAFETERIA moves the men along, old or young, who come to get away from the cold. A half-hour for a cup, they let me sit. Then the manager is at my table. He is nothing but polite. I buy a pastry then, something small. He knows me—I have seen him nearly every day for months now—and by his slight limp I know he is a man of mercy. But business is business.

"What are you reading?" he asks me as he wipes the table with a wet cloth. He touches the saltshaker, nudges the napkins in their holder. I know what this means.

"I'll take a cranberry roll," I say. He flicks the cloth and turns back to the counter.

This is what:

Shall I say, I have gone at dusk through narrow streets
And watched the smoke that rises from the pipes
Of lonely men in shirt-sleeves, leaning out of windows?

Through the magnifier glass the words come forward, huge, two by two. With spectacles, everything is twice enlarged. Still, though,

I am slow to read it. In a half-hour I am finished, could not read more, even if I bought another roll. The boy at the register greets me, smiles when I reach him. "What are you reading today?" he asks, counting out the change.

The books themselves are small and fit in the inside pockets of my coat. I put one in front of each breast, then walk back to see the fish some more. These are the fish I know: the gafftopsail pompano, sixgill shark, the starry flounder with its upturned eyes, queerly migrated. He rests half submerged in sand. His scales are platey and flat-hued. Of everything upward he is wary, of the silvery seabass and the bluefin tuna that pass above him in the region of light and open water. For a life he lies on the bottom of the tank. I look at him. His eyes are dull. They are ugly and an aberration. Above us the bony fishes wheel at the tank's corners. I lean forward to the glass. *"Platichthys stellatus,"* I say to him. The caudal fin stirs. Sand moves and resettles, and I see the black and yellow stripes. "Flatfish," I whisper, "we are, you and I, observers of this life."

"A MAN on our lawn," I say a few nights later in bed.

"Not just that."

I breathe in, breathe out, look up at the ceiling. "What else?"

"When you were out last night he came back."

"He came back."

"Yes."

"What did he do?"

"Looked in at me."

Later, in the early night, when the lights of cars are still passing and the walked dogs still jingle their collar chains out front, I get up quickly from bed and step into the hall. I move fast because this is still possible in short bursts and with concentration. The bed sinks once, then rises. I am on the landing and then downstairs without Francine waking. I stay close to the staircase joists.

In the kitchen I take out my almost blank sheets and set them on the counter. I write standing up because I want to take more than an animal's pose. For me this is futile, but I stand anyway. The page will be blank when I finish. This I know. The dreams I compose are the dreams of others, remembered bits of verse. Songs of greater men than I. In months I have written few more than a hundred words. The pages are stacked, sheets of different sizes.

If I could

one says.

It has never seemed

says another. I stand and shift them in and out. They are mostly blank, sheets from months of nights. But this doesn't bother me. What I have is patience.

FRANCINE knows nothing of the poetry. She's a simple girl, toast and butter. I myself am hardly the man for it: forty years of selling (anything—steel piping, heater elements, dried bananas). Didn't read a book except one on sales. Think victory, the book said. Think *sale*. It's a young man's bag of apples, though; young men in pants that nip at the waist. Ten years ago I left the Buick in the company lot and walked home, dye in my hair, cotton rectangles in the shoulders of my coat. Francine was in the house that afternoon also, the way she is now. When I retired we bought a camper and went on a trip. A traveling salesman retires, so he goes on a trip. Forty miles out of town the folly appeared to me, big as a balloon. To Francine, too. "Frank," she said in the middle of a bend, a prophet turning to me, the camper pushing sixty and rocking in the wind, trucks to our left and right big as trains—"Frank," she said, "these roads must be familiar to you."

So we sold the camper at a loss and a man who'd spent forty years at highway speed looked around for something to do before he died. The first poem I read was in a book on the table in a waiting room. My eyeglasses made half-sense of things.

THESE
are the desolate, dark weeks

I read

when nature in its barrenness
equals the stupidity of man.

Gloom, I thought, and nothing more, but then I reread the words, and suddenly there I was, hunched and wheezing, bald as a trout, and tears were in my eye. I don't know where they came from.

IN THE MORNING an officer visits. He has muscles, mustache, skin red from the cold. He leans against the door frame.

"Can you describe him?" he says.

"It's always dark," says Francine.

"Anything about him?"

"I'm an old woman. I can see that he wears glasses."

"What kind of glasses?"

"Black."

"Dark glasses?"

"Black glasses."

"At a particular time?"

"Always when Frank is away."

"Your husband has never been here when he's come?"

"Never."

"I see." He looks at me. This look can mean several things, perhaps that he thinks Francine is imagining. "But never at a particular time?"

"No."

"Well," he says. Outside on the porch his partner is stamping his feet. "Well," he says again. "We'll have a look." He turns, replaces his cap, heads out to the snowy steps. The door closes. I hear him say something outside.

"Last night—" Francine says. She speaks in the dark. "Last night I heard him on the side of the house."

We are in bed. Outside, on the sill, snow has been building since morning.

"You heard the wind."

"Frank." She sits up, switches on the lamp, tilts her head toward the window. Through a ceiling and two walls I can hear the ticking of our kitchen clock.

"I heard him climbing," she says. She has wrapped her arms about her own waist. "He was on the house. I heard him. He went up the drainpipe." She shivers as she says this. "There was no wind. He went up the drainpipe and then I heard him on the porch roof."

"Houses make noise."

"I heard him. There's gravel there."

I imagine the sounds, amplified by hollow walls, rubber heels on timber. I don't say anything. There is an arm's length between us, cold sheet, a space uncrossed since I can remember.

"I have made the mistake in my life of not being interested in enough people," she says then. "If I'd been interested in more people, I wouldn't be alone now."

"Nobody's alone," I say.

"I mean that if I'd made more of an effort with people I would have friends now. I would know the postman and the Giffords and the Kohlers, and we'd be together in this, all of us. We'd sit in each other's living rooms on rainy days and talk about the children. Instead we've kept to ourselves. Now I'm alone."

"You're not alone," I say.

"Yes, I am." She turns the light off and we are in the dark again. "You're alone, too."

MY HEALTH has gotten worse. It's slow to set in at this age, not the violent shaking grip of death; instead—a slow leak, nothing more.

A bicycle tire: rimless, thready, worn treadless already and now losing its fatness. A war of attrition. The tall camels of the spirit steering for the desert. One morning I realized I hadn't been warm in a year.

And there are other things that go, too. For instance, I recall with certainty that it was on the 23rd of April, 1945, that, despite German counteroffensives in the Ardennes, Eisenhower's men reached the Elbe; but I cannot remember whether I have visited the savings and loan this week. Also, I am unable to produce the name of my neighbor, though I greeted him yesterday in the street. And take, for example, this: I am at a loss to explain whole decades of my life. We have children and photographs, and there is an understanding between Francine and me that bears the weight of nothing less than half a century, but when I gather my memories they seem to fill no more than an hour. Where has my life gone?

It has gone partway to shoddy accumulations. In my wallet are credit cards, a license ten years expired, twenty-three dollars in cash. There is a photograph but it depresses me to look at it, and a poem, half copied and folded into the billfold. The leather is pocked and has taken on the curve of my thigh. The poem is from Walt Whitman. I copy only what I need.

But of all things to do last, poetry is a barren choice. Deciphering other men's riddles while the world is full of procreation and war. A man should go out swinging an axe. Instead, I shall go out in a coffee shop.

But how can any man leave this world with honor? Despite anything he does, it grows corrupt around him. It fills with locks and sirens. A man walks into a store now and the microwaves announce his entry; when he leaves, they make electronic peeks into his coat pockets, his trousers. Who doesn't feel like a thief? I see a policeman now, any policeman, and I feel a fright. And the things I've done wrong in my life haven't been crimes. Crimes of the heart perhaps, but nothing against the state. My soul may turn black but I can wear white trousers at any meeting of men. Have I loved my wife? At one time, yes—in rages and torrents. I've been covered by the pimples of ecstasy and have rooted in the mud of despair; and I've lived for months, for whole years now, as mindless of Francine as a tree is of its mosses.

And this is what kills us, this mindlessness. We sit across the tablecloth now with our medicines between us, little balls and oblongs. We sit, sit. This has become our view of each other, our tableboard apart. We sit.

"AGAIN?" I say.

"Last night."

We are at the table. Francine is making a twisting motion with her fingers. She coughs, brushes her cheek with her forearm, stands suddenly so that the table bumps and my medicines move in the cup.

"Francine," I say.

The half-light of dawn is showing me things outside the window: silhouettes, our maple, the eaves of our neighbor's garage. Francine moves and stands against the glass, hugging her shoulders.

"You're not telling me something," I say.

She sits and makes her pills into a circle again, then into a line. Then she is crying.

I come around the table, but she gets up before I reach her and leaves the kitchen. I stand there. In a moment I hear a drawer open in the living room. She moves things around, then shuts it again. When she returns she sits at the other side of the table. "Sit down," she says. She puts two folded sheets of paper onto the table. "I wasn't hiding them," she says.

"What weren't you hiding?"

"These," she says. "He leaves them."

"He leaves them?"

"They say he loves me."

"Francine."

"They're inside the windows in the morning." She picks one up, unfolds it. Then she reads:

> *Ah, I remember well (and how can I*
> *But evermore remember well) when first*

She pauses, squint-eyed, working her lips. It is a pause of only faint understanding. Then she continues:

> *Our flame began, when scarce we knew what was*
> *The flame we felt.*

When she finishes she refolds the paper precisely. "That's it," she says. "That's one of them."

AT THE AQUARIUM I sit, circled by glass and, behind it, the senseless eyes of fish. I have never written a word of my own poetry but can recite the verse of others. This is the culmination of a life. *Coryphaena hippurus* says the plaque on the dolphin's tank, words more beautiful than any of my own. The dolphin circles, circles, approaches with alarming speed, but takes no notice of, if he even sees, my hands. I wave them in front of his tank. What must he think has become of the sea? He turns and his slippery proboscis nudges the glass. I am every part sore from life.

Ah, silver shrine, here will I take my rest
After so many hours of toil and quest,
A famished pilgrim—saved by miracle.

There is nothing noble for either of us here, nothing between us, and no miracles. I am better off drinking coffee. Any fluid refills the blood. The counter boy knows me and later at the café he pours the cup, most of a dollar's worth. Refills are free but my heart hurts if I drink more than one. It hurts no different from a bone, bruised or cracked. This amazes me.

Francine is amazed by other things. She is mystified, thrown beam ends by the romance. She reads me the poems now at breakfast, one by one. I sit. I roll my pills. "Another came last night," she says, and I see her eyebrows rise. "Another this morning." She reads them as if every word is a surprise. Her tongue touches teeth, shows between lips. These lips are dry. She reads:

Kiss me as if you made believe
You were not sure, this eve,
How my face, your flower, had pursed
Its petals up

That night she shows me the windowsill, second story, rimmed with snow, where she finds the poems. We open the glass. We lean into the air. There is ice below us, sheets of it on the trellis, needles hanging from the drainwork.

"Where do you find them?"

"Outside," she says. "Folded on the lip."

"In the morning?"

"The police should know about this."

"What will they be able to do?"

I step away from the sill. She leans out again, surveying her lands, which are the yard's-width spit of crusted ice along our neighbor's chain link and the three maples out front, now lost their leaves. She peers as if she expects this man to appear. An icy wind comes inside. "Think," she says. "Think. He could come from anywhere."

ONE NIGHT in February, a month after this began, she asks me to stay awake and stand guard until morning. It is almost spring. The earth has reappeared in patches. During the day, at the borders of yards and driveways, I see glimpses of brown—though I know I could be mistaken. I come home early that night, before dusk, and when darkness falls I move a chair by the window downstairs. I draw apart the outer curtain and raise the shade. Francine brings me a pot of tea. She turns out the light and pauses next to me, and as she does, her hand on the chair's backbrace, I am so struck by the proximity of elements—of the night, of the teapot's heat, of the sounds of water outside—that I consider speaking. I want to ask her what has become of us, what has made our breathed air so sorry now, and loveless. But the timing is wrong and in a moment she turns and climbs the stairs. I look out into the night. Later, I hear the closet shut, then our bed creak.

There is nothing to see outside, nothing to hear. This I know. I let hours pass. Behind the window I imagine fish moving down to greet me: broomtail grouper, surfperch, sturgeon with their prehistoric rows of scutes. It is almost possible to see them. The night is full of shapes and bits of light. In it the moon rises, losing the colors of the horizon, so that by early morning it is high and pale. Frost has made a ring around it.

A ringed moon above, and I am thinking back on things. What have I regretted in my life? Plenty of things, mistakes enough to fill the car showroom, then a good deal of the back lot. I've been a man of gains and losses. What gains? My marriage, certainly, though it has been no knee-buckling windfall but more like a split decision in the end, a stock risen a few points since bought. I've certainly enjoyed certain things about the world, too. These are things gone over and over again by the writers and probably enjoyed by everybody who ever lived. Most of them involve air. Early morning air, air after a rainstorm, air through a car window. Sometimes I think the cerebrum is wasted and all we really need is the lower brain, which I've been told is what makes the lungs breathe and the heart beat and what lets us smell pleasant things. What about the poetry? That's another split decision, maybe going the other way if I really made a tally. It's made me melancholy in old age, sad when if I'd stuck with motor homes and the National League standings I don't think I would have been rooting around in regret and doubt at this point. Nothing wrong with sadness, but this is not the real thing—not the death of a child but the feelings of a college student reading *Don Quixote* on a warm afternoon before going out to the lake.

Now, with Francine upstairs, I wait for a night prowler. He will not appear. This I know, but the window glass is ill-blown and makes moving shadows anyway, shapes that change in the wind's rattle. I look out and despite myself am afraid.

Before me, the night unrolls. Now the tree leaves turn yellow in moonshine. By two or three, Francine sleeps, but I get up anyway and change into my coat and hat. The books weigh against my chest. I don gloves, scarf, galoshes. Then I climb the stairs and go into our bedroom, where she is sleeping. On the far side of the bed I see her white hair and beneath the blankets the uneven heave of her chest. I watch the bedcovers rise. She is probably dreaming at this moment. Though we have shared this bed for most of a lifetime I cannot guess what her dreams are about. I step next to her and touch the sheets where they lie across her neck.

"Wake up," I whisper. I touch her cheek, and her eyes open. I know this though I cannot really see them, just the darkness of their sockets.

"Is he there?"

"No."

"Then what's the matter?"

"Nothing's the matter," I say. "But I'd like to go for a walk."

"You've been outside," she says. "You saw him, didn't you?"

"I've been at the window."

"Did you see him?"

"No. There's no one there."

"Then why do you want to walk?" In a moment she is sitting aside the bed, her feet in slippers. "We don't ever walk," she says.

I am warm in all my clothing. "I know we don't," I answer. I turn my arms out, open my hands toward her. "But I would like to. I would like to walk in air that is so new and cold."

She peers up at me. "I haven't been drinking," I say. I bend at the waist, and though my head spins, I lean forward enough so that the effect is of a bow. "Will you come with me?" I whisper. "Will you be queen of this crystal night?" I recover from my bow, and when I look up again she has risen from the bed, and in another moment she has dressed herself in her wool robe and is walking ahead of me to the stairs.

Outside, the ice is treacherous. Snow has begun to fall and our galoshes squeak and slide, but we stay on the plowed walkway long enough to leave our block and enter a part of the neighborhood where I have never been. Ice hangs from the lamps. We pass unfamiliar houses and unfamiliar trees, street signs I have never seen, and as we walk the night begins to change. It is becoming liquor. The snow is banked on either side of the walk, plowed into hillocks at the corners. My hands are warming from the exertion. They are the hands of a younger man now, someone else's fingers in my gloves. They tingle. We take ten minutes to cover a block, but as we move through this neighborhood my ardor mounts. A car approaches and I wave, a boatman's salute, because here we are together on these rare and empty seas. We are nighttime travelers. He flashes his headlamps as he passes, and this fills me to the gullet with celebration and bravery. The night sings to us. I am Bluebeard now, Lindbergh, Genghis Khan.

No, I am not.

I am an old man. My blood is dark from hypoxia, my breaths singsong from disease. It is only the frozen night that is splendid. In it we walk, stepping slowly, bent forward. We take steps the length of table forks. Francine holds my elbow.

I have mean secrets and small dreams, no plans greater than where to buy groceries and what rhymes to read next, and by the time we reach our porch again my foolishness has subsided. My knees and elbows ache. They ache with a mortal ache, tired flesh, the cartilage gone sandy with time. I don't have the heart for dreams. We undress in the hallway, ice in the ends of our hair, our coats stiff from cold. Francine turns down the thermostat. Then we go upstairs and she gets into her side of the bed and I get into mine.

It is dark. We lie there for some time, and then, before dawn, I know she is asleep. It is cold in our bedroom. As I listen to her breathing I know my life is coming to an end. I cannot warm myself. What I would like to tell my wife is this:

What the
imagination
seizes
as beauty must be truth. What holds you
to what you see of me is
that grasp alone.

But I do not say anything. Instead I roll in the bed, reach across, and touch her, and because she is surprised she turns to me.

When I kiss her the lips are dry, cracking against mine, unfamiliar as the ocean floor. But the lips give. They part. I am inside her mouth, and there, still, hidden from the world, as if ruin had forgotten a part, it is wet—Lord! I have the feeling of a miracle. Her tongue comes forward. I do not know myself then, what man I am, who I lie with in embrace. I can barely remember her beauty. She touches my chest and I bite lightly on her lip, spread moisture to her cheek and then kiss her there. She makes something like a sigh. "Frank," she says. "Frank." We are lost now in seas and deserts. My hand finds her fingers and grips them, bone and tendon, fragile things.

Edith Wharton

Letter to W. Morton Fullerton

[The Mount]
August 26 [1908]

Dear, won't you tell me soon the meaning of this silence?

At first I thought it might mean that your sentimental mood had cooled, & that you feared to let me see the change; & I wrote, nearly a month ago, to tell you how natural I should think such a change on your part, & how I hoped that our friendship—so dear to me!—might survive it.—It would have been easy, after that letter, to send a friendly: "Yes, chère amie—" surely, having known me so well all those months, you could have trusted to my understanding it?

But the silence continues! It was not *that* you wanted? For a time I fancied you were too busy & happy to think of writing—perhaps even to glance at my letters when they came. But even so—there are degrees in the lapse from such intimacy as ours into complete silence & oblivion; & if the inclination to write had died out, must not you, who are so sensitive & imaginative, have asked yourself to what conjectures you were leaving me, & how I should suffer at being so abruptly & inexplicably cut off from all news of you?

I re-read your letters the other day, & will not believe that the man who wrote them did not feel them, & did not know enough of the woman to whom they were written to trust to her love & courage, rather than leave her to this aching uncertainty.

What has brought about such a change? Oh, no matter what it is—*only tell me!*

I could take my life up again courageously if I only understood; for whatever those months were to you, to me they were a great gift, a wonderful enrichment; & still I rejoice & give thanks for them! You woke me from a long lethargy, a dull acquiescence in conventional restrictions, a needless self-effacement. If I was awkward & inarticulate it was because, literally, all one side of me was asleep.

I remember, that night we went to [D'Annunzio's play] the "Figlia di Iorio," that in the scene in the cave, where the Figlia sends him back to his mother (I forget all their names), & as he goes he turns & kisses her, & *then she can't let him go*—I remember you turned to me & said laughing: "That's something you don't know anything about."

Well! I *did* know, soon afterward; & if I still remained inexpressive, unwilling, "always drawing away," as you said, it was because I discovered in myself such possibilities of feeling on that side that I feared, if I let you love me too much, I might lose courage when the time came to go away!—Surely you saw this, & understood how I dreaded to be to you, *even for an instant*, the "donna non più giovane" [woman no longer young] who clings & encumbers—how, situated as I was, I thought I could best show my love by refraining—& abstaining? You saw it was all because I loved you?

And when you spoke of your uncertain future, your longing to break away & do the work you really like, didn't you see how my heart *broke* with the thought that, if I had been younger & prettier, everything might have been different—that we might have had together, at least for a short time, a life of exquisite collaborations—a life in which your gifts would have had full scope, & you would have been able to do the distinguished & beautiful things that you ought to do?—Now, I hope, your future has after all arranged itself happily, just as you despaired,—but remember that *those were my thoughts* when you were calling me "conventional" . . .

I never expected to tell you this; but under the weight of this silence I don't know what to say or leave unsaid. After nearly a month my frank tender of friendship remains unanswered. If that was not what you wished, what *is* then your feeling for me? My reason rejects the idea that a man like you, who has felt a warm sympathy for a woman like me, can suddenly, from one day to another, without any act or word on her part, lose even a friendly regard for her, & discard the mere outward signs of consideration by which friendship speaks. And so I am almost driven to conclude that your silence has another meaning, which I have not guessed. If any feeling subsists under it, may these words reach it, & tell you what I felt in silence when we were together!

Yes, dear, I loved you then, & I love you now, as you then wished me to; only I have learned that one must put all the happiness one can into each moment, & I will never again love you "sadly," since that displeases you.

You see I am once more assuming that you *do* care what I feel, in spite of this mystery! How can it be that the sympathy between two people like ourselves, so many-sided, so steeped in imagination, should end from one day to another like a mere "passade"—end by my passing, within a few weeks, utterly out of your memory? By all that I know you are, by all I am myself conscious of being, I declare that I am unable to believe it!

You told me once I should write better for this experience of loving. I felt it to be so, & I came home so fired by the desire that my work should please you! But this incomprehensible silence, the sense of your utter indifference to everything that concerns me, has stunned me. It has come so suddenly . . .

This is the last time I shall write you, dear, unless the strange spell is broken. And my last word is one of tenderness for the friend I love—for the lover I worshipped.

Goodbye, dear.

Oh, I don't want my letters back, dearest! I said that in my other letter only to make it easier for you if you were seeking a transition—

Do you suppose I care what becomes of them if you don't care?

Is it really to my dear friend—to *Henry's [James] friend*—to "dearest Morton"—that I have written this?

Richard Bausch

Letter to the Lady of the House

It's exactly twenty minutes to midnight, on this the eve of my seventieth birthday, and I've decided to address you, for a change, in writing—odd as that might seem. I'm perfectly aware of how many years we've been together, even if I haven't been very good about remembering to commemorate certain dates, certain days of the year. I'm also perfectly aware of how you're going to take the fact that I'm doing this at all, so late at night, with everybody due to arrive tomorrow, the house still unready. I haven't spent almost five decades with you without learning a few things about you that I can predict and describe with some accuracy, though I admit that, as you put it, lately we've been more like strangers than husband and wife. Well, so if we are like strangers, perhaps there are some things I can tell you that you won't have already figured out about the way I feel.

Tonight, we had another one of those long, silent evenings after an argument (remember?) over pepper. We had been bickering all day, really, but at dinner I put pepper on my potatoes and you said that about how I shouldn't have pepper because it always upsets my stomach. I bothered to remark that I used to eat chili peppers for breakfast and if I wanted to put plain old ordinary black pepper on my potatoes, as I had been doing for more than sixty years, that was my privilege. Writing this now, it sounds far more testy than I meant it, but that isn't really the point.

In any case, you chose to overlook my tone. You simply said, "John, you were up all night the last time you had pepper with your dinner."

I said, "I was up all night because I ate green peppers. Not black pepper, but green peppers."

"A pepper is a pepper, isn't it?" you said. And then I started in on you. I got, as you call it, legal with you—pointing out that green peppers are not black pepper—and from there we moved on to an evening of mutual disregard for each other that ended with your decision to go to bed early. The grandchildren will make you tired, and there's still the house to do; you had every reason to want to get some rest, and yet I felt that you were also making a point of getting yourself out of proximity with me, leaving me to my displeasure, with another ridiculous argument settling between us like a fog.

So, after you went to bed, I got out the whiskey and started pouring drinks, and I had every intention of putting myself into a stupor. It was almost my birthday, after all, and—forgive this, it's the way I felt at the time—you had nagged me into an argument and then gone off to bed; the day had ended as so many of our days end now, and I felt, well, entitled. I had a few drinks, without any appreciable effect (though you might well see this letter as firm evidence to the contrary), and then I decided to do something to shake you up. I would leave. I'd make a lot of noise going out the door; I'd take a walk around the neighborhood and make you wonder where I could be. Perhaps I'd go check into a motel for the night. The thought even crossed my mind that I might leave you altogether. I admit that I entertained the thought, Marie. I saw our life together now as the day-to-day round of petty quarreling and tension that it's mostly been over the past couple of years or so, and I wanted out as sincerely as I ever wanted anything.

My God, I wanted an end to it, and I got up from my seat in front of the television and walked back down the hall to the entrance of our room to look at you. I suppose I hoped you'd still be awake so I could tell you of this momentous decision I felt I'd reached. And maybe you were awake: one of our oldest areas of contention being the noise I make—the feather-thin membrane of your sleep that I am always disturbing with my restlessness in the nights. All right. Assuming you were asleep and don't know that I stood in the doorway of our room, I will say that I stood there for perhaps five minutes, looking at you in the half-dark, the shape of your body under the blanket—you really did look like one of the girls when they were little and I used to stand in the doorway of their rooms; your illness last year made you so small again—and, as I said, I thought I had decided to leave you, for your peace as well as mine. I know you have gone to sleep crying, Marie. I know you've felt sorry about things and wished we could find some way to stop irritating each other so much.

Well, of course I didn't go anywhere. I came back to this room and drank more of the whiskey and watched television. It was like all the other nights. The shows came on and ended, and the whiskey began to wear off. There was a little rain shower. I had a moment of the shock of knowing I was seventy. After the rain ended, I did go outside for a few minutes. I stood on the sidewalk and looked at the house. The kids, with their kids, were on the road somewhere between their homes and here. I walked up to the end of the block and back, and a pleasant breeze blew and shook the drops out of the trees. My stomach was bothering me some, and maybe it was the pepper I'd put on my potatoes. It could just as well have been the whiskey. Anyway, as I came back to the house, I began to have the eerie feeling that I had reached the last night of my life. There was this small discomfort in my stomach, and no other physical pang or pain, and I am used to the small ills and side effects of my way of eating and drinking; yet I felt the sense of the end of things more strongly than I can describe. When I stood in the entrance of our room and looked at you again, wondering if I would make it through to the morning, I suddenly found myself trying to think what I would say to you if indeed this *were* the last time I would ever be able to speak to you. And I began to know I would write you this letter.

At least words in a letter aren't blurred by tone of voice, by the old aggravating sound of me talking to you. I began with this and with the idea that, after months of thinking about it, I would at last try to say something to you that wasn't colored by our disaffections. What I have to tell you must be explained in a rather roundabout way.

I've been thinking about my cousin Louise and her husband. When he died and she stayed with us last summer, something brought back to me what is really the only memory of a moment; yet it reached me, that moment, across more than fifty years. As you know, Louise is nine years older than I, and more like an older sister than a cousin. I must have told you at one time or another that I spent some weeks with her, back in 1933, when she first married. The memory I'm talking about comes from that time, and what I have decided I have to tell you comes from that memory.

Father had been dead four years. We were all used to the fact that times were hard and that there was no man in the house, though I suppose I filled that role in some titular way. In any case, when Mother became ill there was the problem of us, her children. Though I was the oldest, I wasn't old enough to stay in the house alone, or to nurse her, either. My grandfather came up with the solution—and everybody went along with it—that I would go to Louise's for a time, and the two girls would go to stay with Grandfather. You'll remember that people did pretty much what that old man wanted them to do.

So we closed up the house, and I got on a train to Virginia. I was a few weeks shy of fourteen years old. I remember that I was not able to believe that anything truly bad would come of Mother's pleurisy, and was consequently glad of the opportunity it afforded me to travel the hundred miles south to Charlottesville, where cousin Louise had moved with her new husband only a month earlier, after her wedding. Because *we* traveled so much at the beginning, you never got to really know Charles when he was young—in 1933 he was a very tall, imposing fellow, with bright red hair and a graceful way of moving that always made me think of athletics, contests of skill. He had worked at the Navy Yard in Washington, and had been laid off in the first months of Roosevelt's New Deal. Louise was teaching in a day school in Charlottesville so they could make ends meet, and Charles was spending most of his time looking for work and fixing up the house. I had only met Charles once or twice before the wedding, but already I admired him and wanted to emulate him. The prospect of spending time in his house, or perhaps going fishing with him in the small streams of central Virginia, was all I thought about on the way down. And I remember that we did go fishing one weekend, that I wound up spending a lot of time with Charles, helping to paint the house and to run water lines under it for indoor plumbing. Oh, I had time with Louise, too—listening to her read from the books she wanted me to be interested in, walking with her around Charlottesville in the evenings and looking at the city as it was then. Or sitting on her small porch and talking about the family, Mother's stubborn illness, the children Louise saw every day at school. But what I want to tell you has to do with the very first day I was there.

I know you think I use far too much energy thinking about and pining away for the past, and I therefore know that I'm taking a risk by talking about this ancient history, and by trying to make you see it. But this all has to do with you and me, my dear, and our late inability to find ourselves in the same room together without bitterness and pain.

That summer, 1933, was unusually warm in Virginia, and the heat, along with my impatience to arrive, made the train almost unbearable. I think it was just past noon when it pulled into the station at Charlottesville, with me hanging out one of the windows, looking for Louise or Charles. It was Charles who had come to meet me. He stood in a crisp-looking seersucker suit, with a straw boater cocked at just the angle you'd expect a young, newly married man to wear a straw boater, even in the middle of economic disaster. I waved at him and he waved back, and I might've jumped out the window if the train had slowed even a little more than it had before it stopped in the shade of the platform. I made my way out, carrying the cloth bag my grandfather had given me for the trip—Mother had said through her rheum that I looked like a carpetbagger—and when I stepped down to shake hands with Charles I noticed that what I thought was a new suit was tattered at the ends of the sleeves.

"Well," he said. "Young John."

I smiled at him. I was perceptive enough to see that his cheerfulness was not entirely effortless. He was a man out of work, after all, and so in spite of himself there was worry in his face, the slightest shadow in an otherwise glad and proud countenance. We walked through the station to the street, and on up the steep hill to the house, which was a small clapboard structure, a cottage, really, with a porch at the end of a short sidewalk lined with flowers—they were marigolds, I think—and here was Louise, coming out of the house, her arms already stretched wide to embrace me. "Lord," she said. "I swear you've grown since the wedding, John." Charles took my bag and went inside.

"Let me look at you, young man," Louise said.

I stood for inspection. And as she looked me over I saw that her hair was pulled back, that a few strands of it had come loose, that it was brilliantly auburn in the sun. I suppose I was a little in love with her. She was grown, and married now. She was a part of what seemed a great mystery to me, even as I was about to enter it, and of course you remember how that feels, Marie, when one is on the verge of things—nearly adult, nearly old enough to fall in love. I looked at Louise's happy, flushed face, and felt a deep ache as she ushered me into her house. I wanted so to be older.

Inside, Charles had poured lemonade for us and was sitting in the easy chair by the fireplace, already sipping his. Louise wanted to show me the house and the backyard—which she had tilled and turned into a small vegetable garden—but she must've sensed how thirsty I was, and so she asked me to sit down and have a cool drink before she showed me the upstairs. Now, of course, looking back on it, I remember that those rooms she was so anxious to show me were meager indeed. They were not much bigger than closets, really, and the paint was faded and dull; the furniture she'd arranged so artfully was coming apart; the pictures she'd put on the walls were prints she'd cut out—magazine covers, mostly—and the curtains over the windows were the same ones that had hung in her childhood bedroom for twenty years. ("Recognize these?" she said with a deprecating smile.) Of course, the quality of her pride had nothing to do with the fineness—or lack of it—in these things, but in the fact that they belonged to her, and that she was a married lady in her own house.

On this day in July, in 1933, she and Charles were waiting for the delivery of a fan they had scrounged enough money to buy from Sears, through the catalogue. There were things they would rather have been doing, especially in this heat, and especially with me there. Monticello wasn't far away, the university was within walking distance, and without too much expense one could ride a taxi to one of the lakes nearby. They had hoped that the fan would arrive before I did, but since it hadn't, and since neither Louise nor Charles was willing to leave the other alone while traipsing off with me that day, there wasn't anything to do but wait around for it. Louise had opened the windows and shut the shades, and we sat in her small living room and drank the lemonade, fanning ourselves with folded parts of Charles's morning newspaper. From time to time an anemic breath of air would move the shades slightly, but then everything grew still again. Louise sat on the arm of Charles's chair, and I sat on the sofa. We talked about pleurisy and, I think, about the fact that Thomas Jefferson had invented the dumbwaiter, how the plumbing at Monticello was at least a century ahead of its time. Charles remarked that it was the spirit of invention that would make a man's career in these days. "That's what I'm aiming for, to be inventive in a job. No matter what it winds up being."

When the lemonade ran out, Louise got up and went into the kitchen to make some more. Charles and I talked about taking a weekend to go fishing. He leaned back in his chair and put his hands behind his head, looking satisfied. In the kitchen, Louise was chipping ice for our glasses, and she began singing something low, for her own pleasure, a barely audible lilting, and Charles and I sat listening. It occurred to me that I was very happy. I had the sense that soon I would be embarked on my own life, as Charles was, and that an attractive woman like Louise would be there with me. Charles yawned and said, "God, listen to that. Doesn't Louise have the loveliest voice?"

AND THAT'S all I have from that day. I don't even know if the fan arrived later, and I have no clear memory of how we spent the rest of the afternoon and evening. I remember Louise singing a song, her husband leaning back in his chair, folding his hands behind his head, expressing his pleasure in his young wife's voice. I remember that I felt quite extraordinarily content just then. And that's all I remember.

But there are, of course, the things we both know: we know they moved to Colorado to be near Charles's parents; we know they never had any children; we know that Charles fell down a shaft at a construction site in the fall of 1957 and was hurt so badly that he never walked again. And I know that when she came to stay with us last summer she told me she'd learned to hate him, and not for what she'd had to help him do all those years. No, it started earlier and was deeper than that. She hadn't minded the care of him—the washing and feeding and all the numberless small tasks she had to perform each and every day, all day—she hadn't minded this. In fact, she thought there was something in her makeup that liked being needed so completely. The trouble was simply that whatever she had once loved in him she had stopped loving, and for many, many years before he died, she'd felt only suffocation when he was near enough to touch her, only irritation and anxiety when he spoke. She said all this, and then looked at me, her cousin, who had been fortunate enough to have children, and to be in love over time, and said, "John, how have you and Marie managed it?"

And what I wanted to tell you has to do with this fact—that while you and I had had one of our whispering arguments only moments before, I felt quite certain of the simple truth of the matter, which is that whatever our complications, we *have* managed to be in love over time.

"Louise," I said.

"People start out with such high hopes," she said, as if I wasn't there. She looked at me. "Don't they?"

"Yes," I said.

She seemed to consider this a moment. Then she said, "I wonder how it happens."

I said, "You ought to get some rest." Or something equally pointless and admonitory.

As she moved away from me, I had an image of Charles standing on the station platform in Charlottesville that summer, the straw boater set at its cocky angle. It was an image I would see most of the rest of that night, and on many another night since.

I CAN ALMOST hear your voice as you point out that once again I've managed to dwell too long on the memory of something that's past and gone. The difference is that I'm not grieving over the past now. I'm merely reporting a memory, so that you might understand what I'm about to say to you.

The fact is, we aren't the people we were even then, just a year ago. I know that. As I know things have been slowly eroding between us for a very long time; we are a little tired of each other, and there are annoyances and old scars that won't be obliterated with a letter—even a long one written in the middle of the night in desperate sincerity, under the influence, admittedly, of a considerable portion of bourbon whiskey, but nevertheless with the best intention and hope: that you may know how, over the course of this night, I came to the end of needing an explanation for our difficulty. We have reached this—place. Everything we say seems rather aggravatingly mindless and automatic, like something one stranger might say to another in any of the thousand circumstances where strangers are thrown together for a time, and the silence begins to grow heavy on their minds, and someone has to say something. Darling, we go so long these days without having anything at all to do with each other, and the children are arriving tomorrow, and once more we'll be in the position of making all the gestures that give them back their parents as they think their parents are, and what I wanted to say to you, what came to me as I thought about Louise and Charles on that day so long ago, when they were young and so obviously glad of each other, and I looked at them and knew it and was happy—what came to me was that even the harsh things that happened to them, even the years of anger and silence, even the disappointment and the bitterness and the wanting not to be in the same room anymore, even all that must have been worth it for such loveliness. At least I am here, at seventy years old, hoping so. Tonight, I went back to our room again and stood gazing at you asleep, dreaming whatever you were dreaming, and I had a moment of thinking how we were always friends, too. Because what I wanted finally to say was that I remember well our own sweet times, our own old loveliness, and I would like to think that even if at the very beginning of our lives together I had somehow been shown that we would end up here, with this longing to be away from each other, this feeling of being trapped together, of being tied to each other in a way that makes us wish for other times, some other place—I would have known enough to accept it all freely for the chance at that love. And if I could, I would do it all again, Marie. All of it, even the sorrow. My sweet, my dear adversary. For everything that I remember.

Philodemus

Poem

Death has torn ten years from us,
Xanthippe, since the day we met
And we had already lost
Thirty, and now grey hairs sprinkle
My head and maturity
Threatens me. But still I love
The sound of your singing voice,
And our thighs locked in a dance,
And my hungry heart still burns . . .
Or, to be brief about it,
I am crazy about you, Xanthippe.

William Butler Yeats

The Wild Old Wicked Man

"Because I am mad about women
I am mad about the hills,"
Said that wild old wicked man
Who travels where God wills,
"Not to die on the straw at home,
Those hands to close these eyes,
That is all I ask, my dear,
From the old man in the skies."
Day-break and a candle end.

"Kind are all your words, my dear,
Do not the rest withhold,
Who can know the year, my dear,
When an old man's blood grows cold.
I have what no young man can have
Because he loves too much.
Words I have that can pierce the heart,
But what can he do but touch?"
Day-break and a candle end.

Then said she to that wild old man
His stout stick under his hand,
"Love to give or to withhold
Is not at my command.
I gave it all to an older man
That old man in the skies.
Hands that are busy with His beads
Can never close those eyes."
Day-break and a candle end.

"Go your ways, O go your ways
I chose another mark,
Girls down on the seashore
Who understand the dark;
Bawdy talk for the fishermen
A dance for the fisher lads;

When dark hangs upon the water
They turn down their beds."
Day-break and a candle end.

"A young man in the dark am I
But a wild old man in the light
That can make a cat laugh, or
Can touch by mother wit
Things hid in their marrow bones
From time long passed away,
Hid from all those warty lads
That by their bodies lay."
Day-break and a candle end.

"All men live in suffering
I know as few can know,
Whether they take the upper road
Or stay content on the low,
Rower bent in his row-boat
Or weaver bent at his loom,
Horsemen erect upon horseback
Or child hid in the womb."
Day-break and a candle end.

"That some stream of lightning
From the old man in the skies

Can burn out that suffering
No right taught man denies.
But a coarse old man am I,
I choose the second-best,
I forget it all awhile
Upon a woman's breast."

Day-break and a candle end.

Edmund Wilson

Anne Miller: "The Situation Has Comic Possibilities"

from The Sixties

JUNE 12. In the morning, went with Anne Miller to the chasm on Sugar River under the railroad bridge, which I don't seem to have described in this journal before and which I wanted to see again. Anne helped me through the stones—I could never have managed without her—she wore tennis shoes and a tennis dress; and when we got to the swimming hole and cataract, she went off from me and with her back to me took off her dress near the falls and went in swimming naked—I saw her slim brownish figure from behind, and she looked very pretty. Two tragedies occurred here: a boy was found drowned—it's not known whether or not he committed suicide—and two girls walking on the trestle were overtaken by the train: one lay down on the ties and let the train pass over; the other, the Erwin girl, I think, tried to hang on with her hands and fell off.

When you get beyond the broken stones, among which grow blue bugloss, buttercups and wood anemone—with a sprinkling of forget-me-nots and violets and occasionally the inevitable beer can, spearmint wrapper, black marks of picnic fires—you find yourself in a high-walled chasm of stratified limestone rock which is feathered with green fern and lined in the cracks with green moss. Birds flit back and forth between the walls. The river runs shallow here with moderate rapids. The cliffs where they overhang are dripping with springs, and across the river, the farther one goes, the more densely they are plumed, grown with trees: ash, feathery hemlock, elm—bushes of sumac. A dead tree droops down over the stream. The cascade is white, rather crooked and ragged. Below it, a brownish froth floats on the swimming hole, and this, and what she thought was a stagnancy of the water in a kind of inlet, made Anne think that it might be polluted and made her dubious about taking the children here. A stretch of primitive landscape invisible and little frequented just off the traffic of Route 12. Above the chasm, against the blue, the coverlet of small dappling clouds crawls slowly below the sky.

Young hell-divers of several summers ago—skim along the surface like aquaplanes, then dive and swim under water for quite a long distance before they suddenly reappear.

WHEN Loren Crosten was driving me that afternoon, a cloud of brown dust was rising from somewhere among the green hills. It was Delio's operations quarrying Dry Sugar River. —The Crostens have bought the place across the way from them, where the children used to annoy them. They found behind the house a horrible dump of garbage, old cars and junk. The inside of the house was more horrible still: an upstairs room where the children apparently simply peed and shat on the floor. The man worked in the furniture factory in Boonville. Loran is going to have the house razed, and they think of having a biological laboratory established there, where the hormones of insects will be studied. —Life at Stanford had, they told me, been quite nerve-racking: bombing of the music school threatened, the windows of their house broken, sleepless nights, calls from the police to look out.

ANNE MILLER: When she came to see me with Ned, after very slight acquaintance, she gave me a big kiss on the mouth. When she came to see me later by herself, we did a great deal of kissing and I proceeded to further intimacies. "I am a very warm person," she said, as if to explain. Anecdote about firemen waving to her and saying "Peace, peace!"—she was evidently making a play on "Piece." I could hardly believe this and made her repeat it on a later occasion. I gave her a good deal of Moselle wine; criticized her poetry: she has no idea of rhyme or meter. We agreed that writing poems is therapeutic—I told her Edna Millay's saying, parodying an ad for apples: "A sonnet a day/Keeps the doctor away." She seems to have been carrying on some kind of affair with someone for two years, trusted me to be discreet, showed me one of his poems, which was just as undistinguished as hers and sounded very much like them. I explained the various kinds of metrical feet and suggested her trying a sonnet. When she did, it didn't come out right—she said that she didn't know why, but when she got to the last lines, they always come out too long. I don't understand her yen for me at my age, and I don't believe it was inspired by her finding that, according to the list in *Esquire*, I was supposed to be one of the hundred most important people in the world; she had already begun to show her interest in me. She is very pretty, brisk, bright—flirtatious but also realistic and direct. I told her that all the men in town must be in love with her—after a moment's silence, "A few," as I had answered when Mary told me that I must have had many beautiful women.

She had had a date with me another afternoon to explore the part of Sugar River beyond the railroad bridge, but called me up and explained that something had gone wrong with her car and she had to have it repaired. Much later, she called me up—it was too late for our walk—and I invited her over for a drink; but she had to get the children's supper. But to my surprise, she very soon called me to say that Ned knew she wanted to see me and had offered to attend to things himself. I found that I was excited in the same way I used to be when I had a rendezvous with a woman—something that hadn't happened to me in years—stopped writing, stopped playing solitaire. But nothing happened except a little kissing—it was then that I gave her most of my instruction in writing verse—rather sloppy, we were drinking more of the Moselle. She is very quick in her replies and in picking things up. The second time I read her poetry, I found that she had already understood how to criticize it herself. She proved to be extremely knowledgeable about flowers, plants, trees and rock formations. Returning from our walk, she had guided me back to the road with her quick attentive observation of what was going to be difficult for me and what I ought to do—after which she produced a bottle of a cheap kind of wine called Ripple, to which the Millers seem to be addicted. We went into the roadside snack restaurant. I followed her example and had what was known as a "sausage sandwich"—which turned out to be terrible, but her merry and friendly companionship could make me enjoy anything. —I had asked her whether her husband didn't object to her seeing other men. "You asked me a strange question," she said on another occasion. "Nothing illicit. I know where I belong." When she came to say goodbye to me the day before I was leaving, I saw the dark top of her head just above the wooden bar across my front windows, as she came past them along the porch with her brisk unself-conscious step.

One day when I had been calling on them, coming out of the house, I found the children playing happily on the lawn—it reminded me of my boyhood at the Collinses'. They turned cartwheels and flip-flops for my benefit. There were dogs, a basset hound who belonged to Ned's brother across the street, their black mongrel and a greyhound that belonged to a neighbor, which she said was an idiot. My impression of a very happy household. I thought that Ned, when I first saw him this summer, seemed a little embarrassed, as if he knew about, or suspected, my necking with Anne; but Rosalind afterwards told me that he had been calling on her, bringing her bottles of Ripple and, she said, making passes at her, and it may have been on this account. Anne has long phalanges in her fingers and toes. I held her feet when she had pulled up her knees on my couch, which did not in the least embarrass her. It seemed natural and pleasantly sensuous. This all seems rather odd for me at 75. The situation has comic possibilities. Three of my old upper row of false teeth came out, and Ned had to put them back. I don't want to spoil, by my attentions to his wife, my relations with the best dentist I have ever had. And he says that I may have to have the same kind of arduous operation on my upper jaw as on my lower.

Samuel Sewall

Judge Sewall Courts Madame Winthrop but Marries the Widow Gibbs

from The Diary of Samuel Sewall

Febr. 6 [1718]. This morning wandering in my mind whether to live a Single or a Married life; I had a sweet and very affectionat Meditation Concerning the Lord Jesus; Nothing was to be objected against his Person, Parentage, Relations, Estate, House, Home! Why did I not resolutely, presently close with Him! And I cry'd mightily to God that He would help me so to doe! . . .

March, 14 [1718]. Deacon Marion comes to me, sits with me a great while in the evening; after a great deal of Discourse about his

Courtship—He told [me] the Olivers said they wish'd I would Court their Aunt [Katherine Brattle Winthrop, the widow of Sewall's friend Chief Justice Wait Still Winthrop]. I said little, but said twas not five Moneths since I buried my dear Wife. Had said before 'twas hard to know whether best to marry again or no; whom to marry. Gave him a book of the Berlin Jewish Converts. [Sewall did marry again, on October 29, 1719, but chose instead Abigail Tilley, who died only six months later.]

Septr 5 [1720]. Mary Hirst goes to Board with Madam Oliver and her Mother Loyd, Going to Son Sewall's I there meet with Madam Winthrop, told her I was glad to meet her there, had not seen her a great while; gave her Mr. Homes's sermon.

Sept. 30 [1720]. Mr. Colman's Lecture: Daughter Sewall acquaints Madam Winthrop that if she pleas'd to be within at 3. p.m. I would wait on her. She answer'd she would be at home.

October 1 [1720]. Satterday, I dine at Mr. Stoddard's: from thence I went to Madam Winthrop's just at 3. Spake to her, saying, my loving wife died so soon and suddenly, 'twas hardly convenient for me to think of Marrying again; however I came to this Resolution, that I would not make my Court to any person without first Consulting with her. Had a pleasant discourse about 7 Single persons sitting in the Fore-seat [September] 29th, viz. Madm Rebekah Dudley, Catharine Winthrop, Bridget Usher, Deliverance Legg, Rebekah Loyd, Lydia Colman, Elizabeth Bellingham. [The front pew of the church was reserved for widows.] She propounded one and another for me; but none would do, said Mrs. Loyd was about her Age.

Octob^r 3. 2 [1720]. Waited on Madam Winthrop again; 'twas a little while before she came in. Her daughter Noyes being there alone with me, I said, I hoped my Waiting on her Mother would not be disagreeable to her. She answer'd she should not be against that that might be for her Comfort. I Saluted her, and told her I perceiv'd I must shortly wish her a good Time; (her mother had told me, she was with Child, and within a Moneth or two of her Time). By and by in came Mr. Airs, Chaplain of the Castle, and hang'd up his Hat, which I was a little startled at, it seeming as if he was to lodge there. At last Madam Winthrop came in. After a considerable time, I went up to her and said, if it might not be inconvenient I desired to speak with her. She assented, and spake of going into another Room; but Mr. Airs and Mrs. Noyes presently rose up, and went out, leaving us there alone. Then I usher'd in Discourse from the names in the Fore-seat; at last I pray'd that Katharine [Mrs. Winthrop] might be the person assign'd for me. She instantly took it up in way of Denyal, as if she had catch'd at an Opportunity to do it, saying she could not do it before she was asked. Said that was her mind unless she should Change it, which she believed she should not; could not leave her Children. I express'd my Sorrow that she should do it so Speedily, pray'd her Consideration, and ask'd her when I should wait upon her agen. She setting no time, I mention'd that day Sennight [a week later]. Gave her Mr. Willard's Fountain open'd with the little print and verses; saying I hop'd if we did well read that book, we should meet together hereafter, if we did not now. She took the Book, and put it in her Pocket. Took Leave.

Oct. 5 [1720]. Midweek, I din'd with the Court; from thence went and visited Cousin Jonathan's wife, Lying in with her little Betty. Gave the Nurse 2^s. Although I had appointed to wait upon her, M^m Winthrop, next Monday, yet I went from my Cousin Sewall's thither about 3. p.m. The Nurse told me Madam dined abroad at her daughter Noyes's, they were to go out together. . . .

[Oct. 6, 1720]. A little after 6 p.m. I went to Madam Winthrop's. She was not within. I gave Sarah Chickering the Maid 2^s, Juno, who brought in wood, 1^s. Afterward the Nurse came in, I gave her 18^d, having no other small Bill. After awhile Dr. Noyes came in with his Mother; and quickly after his wife came in: They sat talking, I think, till eight a-clock. I said I fear'd I might be some Interruption to their Business: Dr. Noyes reply'd pleasantly: He fear'd they might be an Interruption to me, and went away. Madam seem'd to harp upon the same string. Must take care of her Children; could not leave that House and Neighbourhood where she had dwelt so long. I told her she might doe her children as much or more good by bestowing what she laid out in Hous-keeping, upon them. Said her Son would be of Age the 7th of August. I said it might be inconvenient for her to

dwell with her Daughter-in-Law, who must be Mistress of the House. I gave her a piece of Mr. Belcher's Cake and Ginger-Bread wrapped up in a clean sheet of Paper; told her of her Father's kindness to me when Treasurer, and I Constable. My Daughter Judith was gon from me and I was more lonesom—might help to forward one another in our journey to Canaan....

[Oct. 10, 1720]. ... In the Evening I visited Madam Winthrop, who treated me with a great deal of Curtesy; Wine, Marmalade. I gave her the News-Letter about the Thanksgiving Proposals, for sake of the verses for David Jeffries. She tells me Dr. Increase Mather visited her this day, in Mr. Hutchinson's Coach....

[Oct. 12, 1720]. At Mad^{m} Winthrop's Steps I took leave of Capt Hill, &c.

Mrs. Anne Cotton came to door (twas before 8.) said Madam Winthrop was within, directed me into the little Room, where she was full of work behind a Stand; Mrs. Cotton came in and stood. Madam Winthrop pointed to her to set me a Chair. Madam Winthrop's Countenance was much changed from what 'twas on Monday, look'd dark and lowering. At last, the work, (black stuff or Silk) was taken away, I got my Chair in place, had some Converse, but very Cold and indifferent to what 'twas before. Ask'd her to acquit me of Rudeness if I drew off her Glove. Enquiring the reason, I told her twas great odds between handling a dead Goat, and a living Lady. Got it off. I told her I had one Petition to ask of her, that was, that she would take off the Negative she laid on me the third of October; She readily answer'd she could not, and enlarg'd upon it; She told me of it so soon as she could; could not leave her house, children, neighbours, business. I told her she might do som Good to help and support me. . . . Sarah fill'd a Glass of Wine, she drank to me, I to her, She sent Juno home with me with a good Lantern, I gave her 6^{d} and bid her thank her Mistress. In some of our Discourse, I told her I had rather go to the Stone-House adjoining to her, than to come to her against her mind. Told her the reason why I came every other night was lest I should drink too deep draughts of Pleasure. She had talk'd of Canary, her kisses were to me better than the best Canary. . . .

Oct. 13 [1720]. I tell my Son and daughter Sewall, that the Weather was not so fair as I apprehended. . . .

[Oct. 17, 1720]. Monday, Give Mr. Dan Willard, and Mr. Pelatiah Whittemore their Oaths to their Accounts; and Mr. John Briggs to his, as they are Attornys to Dr. Cotton Mather, Administrator to the estate of Nathan Howell deceased. In the Evening I visited Madam Winthrop, who Treated me Courteously, but not in Clean Linen as somtimes. She said, she did not know whether I would come again, or no. I ask'd her how she could so impute inconstancy to me. (I had not visited her since Wednesday night being unable to get over the Indisposition received by the Treatment received that night, and I *must* in it seem'd to sound like a made piece of Formality.) Gave her

this day's Gazett. Heard David Jeffries say the Lord's Prayer, and some other portions of the Scriptures. He came to the door, and ask'd me to go into Chamber, where his Grandmother was tending Little Katee, to whom she had given Physick; but I chose to sit below. Dr. Noyes and his wife came in, and sat a Considerable time; had been visiting Son and dâter Cooper. Juno came home with me.

[Oct. 18, 1720]. Visited Madam Mico, who came to me in a splendid Dress. I said, It may be you have heard of my Visiting Madam Winthrop, her Sister. She answered, Her Sister had told her of it. I ask'd her good Will in the Affair. She answer'd, If her Sister were for it, she should not hinder it. I gave her Mr. Homes's Sermon. She gave me a Glass of Canary, entertain'd me with good Discourse, and a Respectfull Remembrance of my first Wife. I took Leave.

[Oct. 19, 1720]. Midweek, Visited Madam Winthrop; Sarah told me she was at Mr. Walley's, would not come home till late. I gave her Hannah's 3 oranges with her Duty, not knowing whether I should find her or no. Was ready to go home: but said if I knew she was there, I would go thither. Sarah seemd to speak with pretty good Courage, She would be there. I went and found her there, with Mr. Walley and his wife in the little Room below. At 7 a-clock I mentioned going home; at 8. I put on my Coat, and quickly waited on her home. She found occasion to speak loud to the servant, as if she had a mind to be known. Was Courteous to me; but took occasion to speak pretty earnestly about my keeping a Coach: I said 'twould cost

£100. per annum: she said 'twould cost but £40. Spake much against John Winthrop, his false-heartedness. Mr. Eyre came in and sat awhile; I offer'd him Dr. Incr. Mather's Sermons, whereof Mr. Appleton's Ordination-Sermon was one; said he had them already. I said I would give him another. Exit. Came away somewhat late.

Oct. 20 [1720]. Mr. Colman preaches from Luke 15.10. Joy among the Angels: made an Excellent Discourse.

At Council, Col. Townsend spake to me of my Hood: Should get a Wigg. I said twas my chief Ornament: I wore it for sake of the Day. Bro^{r} Odlin, and Sam, Mary, and Jane Hirst dine with us. Promis'd to wait on the Govr about 7. Madam Winthrop not being at Lecture, I went thither first; found her very Serene with her dâter Noyes, Mrs. Dering, and the widow Shipreev sitting at a little Table, she in her arm'd Chair. She drank to me, and I to Mrs. Noyes. After awhile pray'd the favour to speak with her. She took one of the Candles, and went into the best Room, clos'd the shutters, sat down upon the Couch. She told me Madam Usher had been there, and said the Coach must be set on Wheels, and not by Rusting. She spake something of my needing a Wigg. Ask'd me what her Sister said to me. I told her, She said, If her Sister were for it, She would not hinder it. But I told her, she did not say she would be glad to have me for her Brother. Said, I shall keep you in the Cold, and ask her if she would be within tomorrow night, for we had had but a running Feast. She said she could not tell whether she should, or no. I took Leave. As were drinking at the Governour's, he said: In England the Ladies minded little more than that they might have Money, and Coaches to ride in. I said, And New-England brooks its name. At which Mr. Dudley smiled. Govr said they were not quite so bad here.

Oct. 21 [1720]. Friday, My Son, the Minister, came to me p.m. by appointment and we pray one for another in the Old Chamber; more especially respecting my Courtship. About 6. a-clock I go to Madam Winthrop's; Sarah told me her Mistress was gon out, but did not tell me whither she went. She presently order'd me a Fire; so I went in, having Dr. Sibb's Bowels with me to read. I read the first two Sermons, still no body came in: at last about 9. a-clock Mr. Jno Eyre came in; I took the opportunity to say to him as I had done to Mrs. Noyes before, that I hoped my Visiting his Mother would not be disagreeable to him; He answered me with much Respect. When twas after 9. a-clock He of himself said he would go and call her, she was but at one of his Brothers: A while after I heard Madam Winthrop's voice, enquiring something about John. After a good while and Clapping the Garden door twice or thrice, she came in. I mention'd something of the lateness; she banter'd me, and said I was later. She receiv'd me Courteously. I ask'd when our proceedings should be made publick: she said They were like to be no more publick than they were already. Offer'd me no Wine that I remember. I rose up at 11 a-clock to come away, saying I would put on my Coat, she offer'd not to help me. I pray'd her that Juno might light me home, she open'd the Shutter, and said twas pretty light abroad; Juno was weary and gon to bed. So I came hôme by Star-light as well as I could. At my first coming in, I gave Sarah five Shillings. I write Mr. Eyre his Name in his book with the date Octob^{r} 21. 1720. It cost me 8^{s}. Jehovah jireh! Madam told me she had visited M. Mico, Wendell, and Wm Clark of the South [Church].

Octob^{r} 22 [1720]. Dâter Cooper visited me before my going out of Town, staid till about Sun set. I brought her going near as far as the Orange Tree. Coming back, near Leg's Corner, Little David Jeffries saw me, and looking upon me very lovingly, ask'd me if I was going to see his Grandmother? I said, Not to-night. Gave him a penny, and bid him present my Service to his Grandmother.

Octob^{r} 24 [1720]. I went in the Hackny Coach through the Common, stop't at Madam Winthrop's (had told her I would take my departure from thence). Sarah came to the door with Katee in her Arms: but I did not think to take notice of the Child. Call'd her Mistress. I told her, being encourag'd by David Jeffries loving eyes, and sweet Words, I was come to enquire whether she could find in her heart to leave that House and Neighborhood, and go and dwell with me at the South-end; I think she said softly, Not yet. I told her It did not ly in my hands to keep a Coach. If I should, I should be in danger to be brought to keep company with her Neighbour Brooker, (he was a little before sent to prison for Debt). Told her I had an Antipathy against those who would pretend to give themselves; but nothing of their Estate. I would a proportion of my Estate with my self. And I suppos'd she would do so. As to a Perriwig, My best and greatest

Friend, I could not possibly have a greater, began to find me with Hair before I was born, and had continued to do so ever since; and I could not find in my heart to go to another. She commended the book I gave her, Dr. Preston, the Church's Marriage; quoted him saying 'twas inconvenient keeping out of a Fashion commonly used. I said the Time and Tide did circumscribe my Visit. She gave me a Dram of Black-Cherry Brandy, and gave me a lump of the Sugar that was in it. She wish'd me a good Journy. I pray'd God to keep her, and came away. Had a very pleasant Journy to Salem.

[October 31, 1720]. . . . At night I visited Madam Winthrop about 6 p.m. They told me she was gone to Madam Mico's. I went thither and found she was gone; so return'd to her house, read the Epistles to the Galatians, Ephesians in Mr. Eyre's Latin Bible. After the Clock struck 8. I began to read the 103. Psalm. Mr. Wendell came in from his Warehouse. Ask'd me if I were alone? Spake very kindly to me, offer'd me to call Madam Winthrop. I told him, She would be angry, had been at M. Mico's; he help'd me on with my Coat and I came home: left The Gazett in the Bible, which told Sarah of, bid her present my Service to M. Winthrop, and tell her I had been to wait on her if she had been at home.

Novr 1 [1720]. I was so taken up that I could not go if I would.

Novr 2 [1720]. Midweek, went again, and found Mrs. Alden there, who quickly went out. Gave her [Madam Winthrop] about ½ pound of Sugar Almonds, cost 3^s per £. Carried them on Monday. She seem'd pleas'd with them, ask'd what they cost. Spake of giving her a Hundred pounds per annum if I dy'd before her. Ask'd her what sum she would give me, if she should dy first? Said I would give her time to Consider of it. She said she heard as if I had given all to my Children by Deeds of Gift. I told her 'twas a mistake, Point-Judith was mine &c. That in England, I own'd, my Father's desire was that it should go to my eldest Son; 'twas 20£ per annum; she thought 'twas forty. I think when I seem'd to excuse pressing this, she seem'd to think twas best to speak of it; a long winter was coming on. Gave me a Glass or two of Canary.

Novr 4th [1720]. Friday, Went again about 7. a-clock; found there Mr. John Walley and his wife: sat discoursing pleasantly. I shew'd them Isaac Moses's [an Indian] Writing. Madam W. serv'd Comfeits [fruits preserved in vinegar] to us. After a-while a Table was spread, and Supper was set. I urg'd Mr. Walley to Crave a Blessing; but he put it upon me. About 9. they went away. I ask'd Madam what fashioned Necklace I should present her with, She said, None at all. I ask'd her Whereabout we left off last time; mention'd what I had offer'd to give her; Ask'd her what she would give me; She said she could not Change her Condition: She had said so from the beginning; could not be so far from her Children, the Lecture. Quoted the Apostle Paul affirming that a single Life was better than Married. I answer'd That was for the present Distress. Said she had not pleasure in things of that nature as formerly: I said, you are the fitter to make me a Wife. If she held in that mind, I must go home and bewail my Rashness in making more haste than good Speed. However, considering the Supper, I desired her to be within next Monday night, if we liv'd so long. Assented. She charg'd me with saying, that she must put away Juno, if she came to me: I utterly deny'd it, it never came in my heart; yet she insisted upon it; saying it came in upon discourse about the Indian woman that obtained her Freedom this Court. About 10. I said I would not disturb the good orders of her House, and came away. She not seeming pleas'd with my Coming away. Spake to her about David Jeffries, had not seen him.

Monday, Novr 7th [1720]. My son pray'd in the Old Chamber. Our time had been taken up by Son and Daughter Cooper's Visit; so that I only read the 130th and 143. Psalm. Twas on the Account of my Courtship. I went to Mad. Winthrop; found her rocking her little Katee in the Cradle. I excuse'd my Coming so late (near Eight). She set me an arm'd Chair and Cusheon; and so the Cradle was between her arm'd Chair and mine. Gave her the remnant of my Almonds; She did not eat of them as before; but laid them away; I said I came to enquire whether she had alter'd her mind since Friday, or remained of the same mind still. She said, Thereabouts. I told her I loved her, and was so fond [foolish] as to think that she loved me: She said had a great respect for me. I told her, I had made her an offer, without asking any advice; she had so many to advise with, that twas a hindrance. The Fire was come to one short Brand besides the Block, which Brand was set up in end; at last it fell to pieces, and no Recruit was made: She gave me a Glass of Wine. I think I repeated again that I would go home and bewail my Rashness in making more haste than good Speed. I would endeavour to contain myself, and not go on to sollicit her to do that which she could not Consent to. Took leave of her. As came down the steps she bid me have a Care. Treated me Courteously. Told her she had enter'd the 4th year of her Widowhood. I had given her the News-Letter before: I did not bid her draw off her Glove as sometime I had done. Her Dress was not so clean as sometime it had been. Jehovah jireh!

[Nov. 9, 1720]. Midweek, Dine at Bro^{r} Stodard's: were so kind as to enquire of me if they should invite M^{m} Winthrop; I answer'd No. Thank'd my Sister Stoddard for her Courtesie; sat down at the Table Simeon Stoddard esqr, Mad. Stoddard, Samuel Sewall, Mr. Colman, M^{m} Colman, Mr. Cooper, Mrs. Cooper, Mrs. Hannah Cooper, Mr. Samuel Sewall of Brooklin, Mrs. Sewall, Mr. Joseph Sewall, Mrs. Lydia Walley, Mr. William Stoddard. Had a noble Treat. At night our Meeting was at the Widow Belknap's. Gave each one of the Meeting one of Mr. Homes's Sermons, 12 in all; She sent her servant home with me with a Lantern. Mrs. Winthrop's Shutters were open as I pass'd by.

Novr 11 [1720]. Went not to M^{m} Winthrop's. This is the 2^{d} *Withdraw.*

Novr 14 [1720]. Madam Winthrop visits my daughter Sewall with her [granddaughter] Katee.

March, 29th [1722]. Samuel Sewall, and Mrs. Mary Gibbs were joined together in Marriage by the Rev^{d} Mr. William Cooper; Mr. Sewall pray'd once. Mr. Jno Cotton was at Sandwich, sent for by Madam Cotton after her Husband's death.

Stevie Smith

Autumn

He told his life story to Mrs. Courtly
Who was a widow. "Let us get married shortly",
He said, "I am no longer passionate,
But we can have some conversation before it is too late."

Maya Angelou

Many and More

THERE are many and more
who would kiss my hand,
taste my lips,
to my loneliness lend
their bodies' warmth.

I have want of a friend.

There are few, some few,
who would give their names

and fortunes rich
or send first sons
to my ailing bed.

I have need of a friend.

There is one and only one
who will give the air
from his failing lungs
for my body's mend.

And that one is my love.

Michelangelo Buonarroti

Poem

Now in this chill season
of my age no longer green
Still flares beyond all reason
the flame unspent, if lean.

thus Love who doth remember
that aimed at a gentle heart
the blow hits true, ignites the ember,
And so he draws with art

His bow . . . and all is green again!
Green green the dry place!
At the merest glimpse of a lovely face
Green the bark and green the fen!

And this ultimate arrow, barbed, astounding,
brings me down to a second Fall
More painful than my first wounding
More dolorous, dangerous than them all.

Anton Chekhov

The Lady with the Pet Dog

A NEW PERSON, it was said, had appeared on the esplanade: a lady with a pet dog. Dmitry Dmitrich Gurov, who had spent a fortnight at Yalta and had got used to the place, had also begun to take an interest in new arrivals. As he sat in Vernet's confectionery shop, he saw, walking on the esplanade, a fair-haired young woman of medium height, wearing a beret; a white Pomeranian was trotting behind her.

And afterwards he met her in the public garden and in the square several times a day. She walked alone, always wearing the same beret and always with the white dog; no one knew who she was and everyone called her simply "the lady with the pet dog."

"If she is here alone without husband or friends," Gurov reflected, "it wouldn't be a bad thing to make her acquaintance."

He was under forty, but he already had a daughter twelve years old, and two sons at school. They had found a wife for him when he was very young, a student in his second year, and by now she seemed half as old again as he. She was a tall, erect woman with dark eyebrows, stately and dignified and, as she said of herself, intellectual. She read a great deal, used simplified spelling in her letters, called her husband, not Dmitry, but Dimitry, while he privately considered her of limited intelligence, narrow-minded, dowdy, was afraid of her, and did not like to be at home. He had begun being unfaithful to her long ago—had been unfaithful to her often and, probably for that reason, almost always spoke ill of women, and when they were talked of in his presence used to call them "the inferior race."

It seemed to him that he had been sufficiently tutored by bitter experience to call them what he pleased, and yet he could not have lived without "the inferior race" for two days together. In the company of men he was bored and ill at ease, he was chilly and uncommunicative with them; but when he was among women he felt free, and knew what to speak to them about and how to comport himself; and even to be silent with them was no strain on him. In his appearance, in his character, in his whole make-up there was something attractive and elusive that disposed women in his favor and allured them. He knew that, and some force seemed to draw him to them, too.

Oft-repeated and really bitter experience had taught him long ago that with decent people—particularly Moscow people—who are irresolute and slow to move, every affair which at first seems a light and charming adventure inevitably grows into a whole problem of extreme complexity, and in the end a painful situation is created. But at every new meeting with an interesting woman this lesson of experience seemed to slip from his memory, and he was eager for life, and everything seemed so simple and diverting.

One evening while he was dining in the public garden the lady in the beret walked up without haste to take the next table. Her expression, her gait, her dress, and the way she did her hair told him that she belonged to the upper class, that she was married, that she was in Yalta for the first time and alone, and that she was bored there. The stories told of the immorality in Yalta are to a great extent untrue; he despised them, and knew that such stories were made up for the most part by persons who would have been glad to sin themselves if they had had the chance; but when the lady sat down at the next table three paces from him, he recalled these stories of easy conquests, of trips to the mountains, and the tempting thought of a swift, fleeting liaison, a romance with an unknown woman of whose very name he was ignorant suddenly took hold of him.

He beckoned invitingly to the Pomeranian, and when the dog approached him, shook his finger at it. The Pomeranian growled; Gurov threatened it again.

The lady glanced at him and at once dropped her eyes.

"He doesn't bite," she said, and blushed.

"May I give him a bone?" he asked; and when she nodded he inquired affably, "Have you been in Yalta long?"

"About five days."

"And I am dragging out the second week here."

There was a short silence.

"Time passes quickly, and yet it is so dull here!" she said, not looking at him.

"It's only the fashion to say it's dull here. A provincial will live in Belyov or Zhizdra and not be bored, but when he comes here it's 'Oh, the dullness! Oh, the dust!' One would think he came from Granada."

She laughed. Then both continued eating in silence, like strangers, but after dinner they walked together and there sprang up between them the light banter of people who are free and contented, to whom it does not matter where they go or what they talk about. They walked and talked of the strange light on the sea: the water was a soft, warm, lilac color, and there was a golden band of moonlight upon it. They talked of how sultry it was after a hot day. Gurov told her that he was a native of Moscow, that he had studied languages and literature at the university, but had a post in a bank; that at one time he had trained to become an opera singer but had given it up, that he owned two houses in Moscow. And he learned from her that she had grown up in Petersburg, but had lived in S— since her marriage two years previously, that she was going to stay in Yalta for about another month, and that her husband, who needed a rest, too, might perhaps come to fetch her. She was not certain whether her husband was a member of a Government Board or served on a *Zemstvo Council*, and this amused her. And Gurov learned too that her name was Anna Sergeyevna.

Afterwards in his room at the hotel he thought about her—and was certain that he would meet her the next day. It was bound to happen. Getting into bed he recalled that she had been a schoolgirl only recently, doing lessons like his own daughter; he thought how much timidity and angularity there was still in her laugh and her manner of talking with a stranger. It must have been the first time in her life that she was alone in a setting in which she was followed, looked at, and spoken to for one secret purpose alone, which she could hardly fail to guess. He thought of her slim, delicate throat, her lovely gray eyes.

"There's something pathetic about her, though," he thought, and dropped off.

II

A WEEK HAD passed since they had struck up an acquaintance. It was a holiday. It was close indoors, while in the street the wind whirled the dust about and blew people's hats off. One was thirsty all day, and Gurov often went into the restaurant and offered Anna Sergeyevna a soft drink or ice cream. One did not know what to do with oneself.

In the evening when the wind had abated they went out on the pier to watch the steamer come in. There were a great many people walking about the dock; they had come to welcome someone and they were carrying bunches of flowers. And two peculiarities of a festive Yalta crowd stood out: the elderly ladies were dressed like young ones and there were many generals.

Owing to the choppy sea, the steamer arrived late, after sunset, and it was a long time tacking about before it put in at the pier. Anna Sergeyevna peered at the steamer and the passengers through her lorgnette as though looking for acquaintances, and whenever she turned to Gurov her eyes were shining. She talked a great deal and asked questions jerkily, forgetting the next moment what she had asked; then she lost her lorgnette in the crush.

The festive crowd began to disperse; it was now too dark to see people's faces; there was no wind any more, but Gurov and Anna Sergeyevna still stood as though waiting to see someone else come off the steamer. Anna Sergeyevna was silent now, and sniffed her flowers without looking at Gurov.

"The weather has improved this evening," he said. "Where shall we go now? Shall we drive somewhere?"

She did not reply.

Then he looked at her intently, and suddenly embraced her and kissed her on the lips, and the moist fragrance of her flowers enveloped him; and at once he looked round him anxiously, wondering if anyone had seen them.

"Let us go to your place," he said softly. And they walked off together rapidly.

The air in her room was close and there was the smell of the perfume she had bought at the Japanese shop. Looking at her, Gurov thought: "What encounters life offers!" From the past he preserved the memory of carefree, good-natured women whom love made gay and who were grateful to him for the happiness he gave them, however brief it might be; and of women like his wife who loved without sincerity, with too many words, affectedly, hysterically, with an expression that it was not love or passion that engaged them but something more significant; and of two or three others, very beautiful, frigid women, across whose faces would suddenly flit a rapacious expression—an obstinate desire to take from life more than it could give, and these were women no longer young, capricious, unreflecting, domineering, unintelligent, and when Gurov grew cold to them their beauty aroused his hatred, and the lace on their lingerie seemed to him to resemble scales.

But here there was the timidity, the angularity of inexperienced youth, a feeling of awkwardness; and there was a sense of embarrassment, as though someone had suddenly knocked at the door. Anna Sergeyevna, "the lady with the pet dog," treated what had happened in a peculiar way, very seriously, as though it were her fall—so it seemed, and this was odd and inappropriate. Her features drooped and faded, and her long hair hung down sadly on either side of her face; she grew pensive and her dejected pose was that of a Magdalene in a picture by an old master.

"It's not right," she said. "You don't respect me now, you first of all."

There was a watermelon on the table. Gurov cut himself a slice and began eating it without haste. They were silent for at least half an hour.

There was something touching about Anna Sergeyevna; she had the purity of a well-bred, naive woman who has seen little of life. The single candle burning on the table barely illumined her face, yet it was clear that she was unhappy.

"Why should I stop respecting you, darling?" asked Gurov. "You don't know what you're saying."

"God forgive me," she said, and her eyes filled with tears. "It's terrible."

"It's as though you were trying to exonerate yourself."

"How can I exonerate myself? No. I am a bad, low woman; I despise myself and I have no thought of exonerating myself. It's not my husband but myself I have deceived. And not only just now; I have been deceiving myself for a long time. My husband may be a good, honest man, but he is a flunkey! I don't know what he does, what his work is, but I know he is a flunkey! I was twenty when I married him. I was tormented by curiosity; I wanted something better. 'There must be a different sort of life,' I said to myself. I wanted to live! To live, to live! Curiosity kept eating at me—you don't understand it, but I swear to God I could no longer control myself; something was going on in me: I could not be held back. I told my husband I was ill, and came here. And here I have been walking about as though in a daze, as though I were mad; and now I have become a vulgar, vile woman whom anyone may despise."

Gurov was already bored with her; he was irritated by her naive tone, by her repentance, so unexpected and so out of place; but for the tears in her eyes he might have thought she was joking or play-acting.

"I don't understand, my dear," he said softly. "What do you want?"

She hid her face on his breast and pressed close to him.

"Believe me, believe me, I beg you," she said, "I love honesty and purity, and sin is loathsome to me; I don't know what I'm doing. Simple people say, 'The Evil One has led me astray.' And I may say of myself now that the Evil One has led me astray."

"Quiet, quiet," he murmured.

He looked into her fixed, frightened eyes, kissed her, spoke to her softly and affectionately, and by degrees she calmed down, and her gaiety returned; both began laughing.

Afterwards when they went out there was not a soul on the esplanade. The town with its cypresses looked quite dead, but the sea was still sounding as it broke upon the beach; a single launch was rocking on the waves and on it a lantern was blinking sleepily.

They found a cab and drove to Oreanda.

"I found out your surname in the hall just now: it was written on the board—von Dideritz," said Gurov. "Is your husband German?"

"No; I believe his grandfather was German, but he is Greek Orthodox himself."

At Oreanda they sat on a bench not far from the church, looked down at the sea, and were silent. Yalta was barely visible through the morning mist; white clouds rested motionlessly on the mountain-tops. The leaves did not stir on the trees, cicadas twanged, and the monotonous muffled sound of the sea that rose from below spoke of the peace, the eternal sleep awaiting us. So it rumbled below when there was no Yalta, no Oreanda here; so it rumbles now, and it will rumble as indifferently and as hollowly when we are no more. And in this constancy, in this complete indifference to the life and death of each of us, there lies, perhaps, a pledge of our eternal salvation, of the unceasing advance of life upon earth, of unceasing movement towards perfection. Sitting beside a young woman who in the dawn seemed so lovely, Gurov, soothed and spellbound by these magical surroundings—the sea, the mountains, the clouds, the wide sky—thought how everything is really beautiful in this world when one reflects: everything except what we think or do ourselves when we forget the higher aims of life and our own human dignity.

A man strolled up to them—probably a guard—looked at them and walked away. And this detail, too, seemed so mysterious and beautiful. They saw a steamer arrive from Feodosia, its lights extinguished in the glow of dawn.

"There is dew on the grass," said Anna Sergeyevna, after a silence.

"Yes, it's time to go home."

They returned to the city.

Then they met every day at twelve o'clock on the esplanade, lunched and dined together, took walks, admired the sea. She complained that she slept badly, that she had palpitations, asked the same questions, troubled now by jealousy and now by the fear that he did not respect her sufficiently. And often in the square or the public garden, when there was no one near them, he suddenly drew her to him and kissed her passionately. Complete idleness, these kisses in broad daylight exchanged furtively in dread of someone's seeing them, the heat, the smell of the sea, and the continual flitting before his eyes of idle, well-dressed, well-fed people, worked a complete change in him; he kept telling Anna Sergeyevna how beautiful she was, how seductive, was urgently passionate; he would not move a step away from her, while she was often pensive and continually pressed him to confess that he did not respect her, did not love her in the least, and saw in her nothing but a common woman. Almost every evening rather late they drove somewhere out of town, to Oreanda or to the waterfall; and the excursion was always a success, the scenery invariably impressed them as beautiful and magnificent.

They were expecting her husband, but a letter came from him saying that he had eye-trouble, and begging his wife to return home as soon as possible. Anna Sergeyevna made haste to go.

"It's a good thing I am leaving," she said to Gurov. "It's the hand of Fate!"

She took a carriage to the railway station, and he went with her. They were driving the whole day. When she had taken her place in the express, and when the second bell had rung, she said, "Let me look at you once more—let me look at you again. Like this."

She was not crying but was so sad that she seemed ill, and her face was quivering.

"I shall be thinking of you—remembering you," she said. "God bless you; be happy. Don't remember evil against me. We are parting forever—it has to be, for we ought never to have met. Well, God bless you."

The train moved off rapidly, its lights soon vanished, and a minute later there was no sound of it, as though everything had conspired to end as quickly as possible that sweet trance, that madness. Left alone on the platform, and gazing into the dark distance, Gurov listened to the twang of the grasshoppers and the hum of the telegraph wires, feeling as though he had just waked up. And he reflected, musing, that there had now been another episode or adventure in his life, and it, too, was at an end, and nothing was left of it but a memory. He was moved, sad, and slightly remorseful: this young woman whom he would never meet again had not been happy with him; he had been warm and affectionate with her, but yet in his manner, his tone, and his caresses there had been a shade of light irony, the slightly coarse arrogance of a happy male who was, besides, almost twice her age. She had constantly called him kind, exceptional, high-minded; obviously he had seemed to her different from what he really was, so he had involuntarily deceived her.

Here at the station there was already a scent of autumn in the air; it was a chilly evening.

"It is time for me to go north, too," thought Gurov as he left the platform. "High time!"

III

At home in Moscow the winter routine was already established: the stoves were heated, and in the morning it was still dark when the children were having breakfast and getting ready for school, and the nurse would light the lamp for a short time. There were frosts already. When the first snow falls, on the first day the sleighs are out, it is pleasant to see the white earth, the white roofs; one draws easy, delicious breaths, and the season brings back the days of one's youth. The old limes and birches, white with hoar-frost, have a good-natured look; they are closer to one's heart than cypresses and palms, and near them one no longer wants to think of mountains and the sea.

Gurov, a native of Moscow, arrived there on a fine frosty day, and when he put on his fur coat and warm gloves and took a walk along Petrovka, and when on Saturday night he heard the bells ringing, his recent trip and the places he had visited lost all charm for him. Little by little he became immersed in Moscow life, greedily read three newspapers a day, and declared that he did not read the Moscow papers on principle. He already felt a longing for restaurants, clubs, formal dinners, anniversary celebrations, and it flattered him to entertain distinguished lawyers and actors, and to play cards with a professor at the physicians' club. He could eat a whole portion of meat stewed with pickled cabbage and served in a pan, Moscow style.

A month or so would pass and the image of Anna Sergeyevna, it seemed to him, would become misty in his memory, and only from time to time he would dream of her with her touching smile as he dreamed of others. But more than a month went by, winter came into its own, and everything was still clear in his memory as though he had parted from Anna Sergeyevna only yesterday. And his memories glowed more and more vividly. When in the evening stillness the voices of his children preparing their lessons reached his study, or when he listened to a song or to an organ playing in a restaurant, or when the storm howled in the chimney, suddenly everything would rise up in his memory: what had happened on the pier and the early morning with the mist on the mountains, and the steamer coming from Feodosia, and the kisses. He would pace about his room a long time, remembering and smiling; then his memories passed into reveries, and in his imagination the past would mingle with what was to come. He did not dream of Anna Sergeyevna, but she followed him about everywhere and watched him. When he shut his eyes he saw her before him as though she were there in the flesh, and she seemed to him lovelier, younger, tenderer than she had been, and he imagined himself a finer man than he had been in Yalta. Of evenings she peered out at him from the bookcase, from the fireplace, from the corner—he heard her breathing, the caressing rustle of her clothes. In the street he followed the women with his eyes, looking for someone who resembled her.

Already he was tormented by a strong desire to share his memories with someone. But in his home it was impossible to talk of his love, and he had no one to talk to outside; certainly he could not confide in his tenants or in anyone at the bank. And what was there to talk about? He hadn't loved her then, had he? Had there been anything beautiful, poetical, edifying, or simply interesting in his relations with Anna Sergeyevna? And he was forced to talk vaguely of love, of women, and no one guessed what he meant; only his wife would twitch her black eyebrows and say, "The part of a philanderer does not suit you at all, Dimitry."

One evening, coming out of the physicians' club with an official with whom he had been playing cards, he could not resist saying:

"If you only knew what a fascinating woman I became acquainted with at Yalta!"

The official got into his sledge and was driving away, but turned suddenly and shouted:

"Dmitry Dmitrich!"

"What is it?"

"You were right this evening: the sturgeon was a bit high."

These words, so commonplace, for some reason moved Gurov to indignation, and struck him as degrading and unclean. What savage manners, what mugs! What stupid nights, what dull, humdrum days! Frenzied gambling, gluttony, drunkenness, continual talk always about the same things! Futile pursuits and conversations always about the same topics take up the better part of one's time, the better part of one's strength, and in the end there is left a life clipped and wingless, an absurd mess, and there is no escaping or getting away from it—just as though one were in a madhouse or a prison.

Gurov, boiling with indignation, did not sleep all night. And he had a headache all the next day. And the following nights too he slept badly; he sat up in bed, thinking, or paced up and down his room. He was fed up with his children, fed up with the bank; he had no desire to go anywhere or to talk of anything.

In December during the holidays he prepared to take a trip and told his wife he was going to Petersburg to do what he could for a young friend—and he set off for S—. What for? He did not know, himself. He wanted to see Anna Sergeyevna and talk with her, to arrange a rendezvous if possible.

He arrived at S— in the morning, and at the hotel took the best room, in which the floor was covered with gray army cloth, and on the table there was an inkstand, gray with dust and topped by a figure on horseback, its hat in its raised hand and its head broken off. The porter gave him the necessary information: von Dideritz lived in a house of his own on Staro-Goncharnaya Street, not far from the hotel: he was rich and lived well and kept his own horses; everyone in the town knew him. The porter pronounced the name: "Dridiritz."

Without haste Gurov made his way to Staro-Goncharnaya Street and found the house. Directly opposite the house stretched a long gray fence studded with nails.

"A fence like that would make one run away," thought Gurov, looking now at the fence, now at the windows of the house.

He reflected: this was a holiday, and the husband was apt to be at home. And in any case, it would be tactless to go into the house and disturb her. If he were to send her a note, it might fall into her husband's hands, and that might spoil everything. The best thing was to rely on chance. And he kept walking up and down the street and along the fence, waiting for the chance. He saw a beggar go in at the gate and heard the dogs attack him; then an hour later he heard a piano, and the sound came to him faintly and indistinctly. Probably it was Anna Sergeyevna playing. The front door opened suddenly, and an old woman came out, followed by the familiar white Pomeranian. Gurov was on the point of calling to the dog, but his heart began beating violently, and in his excitement he could not remember the Pomeranian's name.

He kept walking up and down, and hated the gray fence more and more, and by now he thought irritably that Anna Sergeyevna had forgotten him, and was perhaps already diverting herself with another man, and that that was very natural in a young woman who from morning till night had to look at that damn fence. He went back to his hotel room and sat on the couch for a long while, not knowing what to do, then he had dinner and a long nap.

"How stupid and annoying all this is!" he thought when he woke and looked at the dark windows: it was already evening. "Here I've had a good sleep for some reason. What am I going to do at night?"

He sat on the bed, which was covered with a cheap gray blanket of the kind seen in hospitals, and he twitted himself in his vexation:

"So there's your lady with the pet dog. There's your adventure. A nice place to cool your heels in."

That morning at the station a playbill in large letters had caught his eye. *The Geisha* was to be given for the first time. He thought of this and drove to the theater.

"It's quite possible that she goes to first nights," he thought.

The theater was full. As in all provincial theaters, there was a haze above the chandelier, the gallery was noisy and restless; in the front row, before the beginning of the performance the local dandies were standing with their hands clasped behind their backs; in the Governor's box the Governor's daughter, wearing a boa, occupied the front seat, while the Governor himself hid modestly behind the portiere and only his hands were visible; the curtain swayed; the orchestra was a long time tuning up. While the audience were coming in and taking their seats, Gurov scanned the faces eagerly.

Anna Sergeyevna, too, came in. She sat down in the third row, and when Gurov looked at her his heart contracted, and he understood clearly that in the whole world there was no human being so near, so precious, and so important to him; she, this little, undistinguished woman, lost in a provincial crowd, with a vulgar lorgnette in her hand, filled his whole life now, was his sorrow and his joy, the only happiness that he now desired for himself, and to the sounds of the bad orchestra, of the miserable local violins, he thought how lovely she was. He thought and dreamed.

A young man with small side-whiskers, very tall and stooped, came in with Anna Sergeyevna and sat down beside her; he nodded his head at every step and seemed to be bowing continually. Probably this was the husband whom at Yalta, in an access of bitter feeling, she had called a flunkey. And there really was in his lanky figure, his side-whiskers, his small bald patch, something of a flunkey's retiring manner; his smile was mawkish, and in his buttonhole there was an academic badge like a waiter's number.

During the first intermission the husband went out to have a smoke; she remained in her seat. Gurov, who was also sitting in the orchestra, went up to her and said in a shaky voice, with a forced smile:

"Good evening!"

She glanced at him and turned pale, then looked at him again in horror, unable to believe her eyes, and gripped the fan and the lorgnette tightly together in her hands, evidently trying to keep herself from fainting. Both were silent. She was sitting, he was standing, frightened by her distress and not daring to take a seat beside her. The violins and the flute that were being tuned up sang out. He suddenly felt frightened: it seemed as if all the people in the boxes were looking at them. She got up and went hurriedly to the exit; he followed her, and both of them walked blindly along the corridors and up and down stairs, and figures in the uniforms prescribed for magistrates, teachers, and officials of the Department of Crown Lands, all wearing badges, flitted before their eyes, as did also ladies, and fur coats on hangers; they were conscious of drafts and the smell of stale tobacco. And Gurov, whose heart was beating violently, thought:

"Oh, Lord! Why are these people here and this orchestra!"

And at that instant he suddenly recalled how when he had seen Anna Sergeyevna off at the station he had said to himself that all was over between them and that they would never meet again. But how distant the end still was!

On the narrow, gloomy staircase over which it said "To the Amphitheatre," she stopped.

"How you frightened me!" she said, breathing hard, still pale and stunned. "Oh, how you frightened me! I am barely alive. Why did you come? Why?"

"But do understand, Anna, do understand—" he said hurriedly, under his breath. "I implore you, do understand—"

She looked at him with fear, with entreaty, with love; she looked at him intently, to keep his features more distinctly in her memory.

"I suffer so," she went on, not listening to him. "All this time I have been thinking of nothing but you; I live only by the thought of you. And I wanted to forget, to forget; but why, oh, why have you come?"

On the landing above them two high school boys were looking down and smoking, but it was all the same to Gurov; he drew Anna Sergeyevna to him and began kissing her face and her hands.

"What are you doing, what are you doing!" she was saying in horror, pushing him away. "We have lost our senses. Go away today; go away at once— I conjure you by all that is sacred, I implore you— People are coming this way!"

Someone was walking up the stairs.

"You must leave," Anna Sergeyevna went on in a whisper. "Do you hear, Dmitry Dmitrich? I will come and see you in Moscow. I have never been happy; I am unhappy now, and I never, never shall be happy, never! So don't make me suffer still more! I swear I'll come to Moscow. But now let us part. My dear, good, precious one, let us part!"

She pressed his hand and walked rapidly downstairs, turning to look round at him, and from her eyes he could see that she really was unhappy. Gurov stood for a while, listening, then when all grew quiet, he found his coat and left the theater.

IV

AND ANNA Sergeyevna began coming to see him in Moscow. Once every two or three months she left S—, telling her husband that she was going to consult a doctor about a woman's ailment from which she was suffering—and her husband did and did not believe her. When she arrived in Moscow she would stop at the Slavyansky Bazar Hotel, and at once send a man in a red cap to Gurov. Gurov came to see her, and no one in Moscow knew of it.

Once he was going to see her in this way on a winter morning (the messenger had come the evening before and not found him in). With him walked his daughter, whom he wanted to take to school: it was on the way. Snow was coming down in big wet flakes.

"It's three degrees above zero, and yet it's snowing," Gurov was saying to his daughter. "But this temperature prevails only on the surface of the earth; in the upper layers of the atmosphere there is quite a different temperature."

"And why doesn't it thunder in winter, papa?"

He explained that, too. He talked, thinking all the while that he was on his way to a rendezvous, and no living soul knew of it, and probably no one would ever know. He had two lives: an open one, seen and known by all who needed to know it, full of conventional truth and conventional falsehood, exactly like the lives of his friends and acquaintances; and another life that went on in secret. And through some strange, perhaps accidental, combination of circumstances, everything that was of interest and importance to him, everything that was essential to him, everything about which he felt sincerely and did not deceive himself, everything that constituted the core of his life, was going on concealed from others; while all that was false, the shell in which he hid to cover the truth—his work at the bank, for instance, his discussions at the club, his references to the "inferior race," his appearances at anniversary celebrations with his wife—all that went on in the open. Judging others by himself, he did not believe what he saw, and always fancied that every man led his real, most interesting life under cover of secrecy as under cover of night. The personal life of every individual is based on secrecy, and perhaps it is partly for that reason that civilized man is so nervously anxious that personal privacy should be respected.

Having taken his daughter to school, Gurov went on to the Slavyansky Bazar Hotel. He took off his fur coat in the lobby, went upstairs, and knocked gently at the door. Anna Sergeyevna, wearing his favorite gray dress, exhausted by the journey and by waiting, had been expecting him since the previous evening. She was pale, and looked at him without a smile, and he had hardly entered when she flung herself on his breast. Their kiss was a long, lingering one, as though they had not seen one another for two years.

"Well, darling, how are you getting on there?" he asked. "What news?"

"Wait; I'll tell you in a moment— I can't speak."

She could not speak; she was crying. She turned away from him, and pressed her handkerchief to her eyes.

"Let her have her cry; meanwhile I'll sit down," he thought, and he seated himself in an armchair.

Then he rang and ordered tea, and while he was having his tea she remained standing at the window with her back to him. She was crying out of sheer agitation, in the sorrowful consciousness that their life was so sad; that they could only see each other in secret and had to hide from people like thieves! Was it not a broken life?

"Come, stop now, dear!" he said.

It was plain to him that this love of theirs would not be over soon, that the end of it was not in sight. Anna Sergeyevna was growing more and more attached to him. She adored him, and it was unthinkable to tell her that their love was bound to come to an end some day; besides, she would not have believed it!

He went up to her and took her by the shoulders, to fondle her and say something diverting, and at that moment he caught sight of himself in the mirror.

His hair was already beginning to turn gray. And it seemed odd to him that he had grown so much older in the last few years, and lost his looks. The shoulders on which his hands rested were warm and heaving. He felt compassion for this life, still so warm and lovely, but probably already about to begin to fade and wither like his own. Why did she love him so much? He always seemed to women different from what he was, and they loved in him not himself, but the man whom their imagination created and whom they had been eagerly seeking all their lives; and afterwards, when they saw their mistake, they loved him nevertheless. And not one of them had been happy with him. In the past he had met women, come together with them, parted from them, but he had never once loved; it was anything you please, but not love. And only now when his head was gray he had fallen in love, really, truly—for the first time in his life.

Anna Sergeyevna and he loved each other as people do who are very close and intimate, like man and wife, like tender friends; it seemed to them that Fate itself had meant them for one another, and they could not understand why he had a wife and she a husband; and it was as though they were a pair of migratory birds, male and female, caught and forced to live in different cages. They forgave each other what they were ashamed of in their past, they forgave everything in the present, and felt that this love of theirs had altered them both.

Formerly in moments of sadness he had soothed himself with whatever logical arguments came into his head, but now he no longer cared for logic; he felt profound compassion, he wanted to be sincere and tender.

"Give it up now, my darling," he said. "You've had your cry;

that's enough. Let us have a talk now, we'll think up something." Then they spent a long time taking counsel together, they talked of how to avoid the necessity for secrecy, for deception, for living in different cities, and not seeing one another for long stretches of time. How could they free themselves from these intolerable fetters?

"How? How?" he asked, clutching his head. "How?"

And it seemed as though in a little while the solution would be found, and then a new and glorious life would begin; and it was clear to both of them that the end was still far off, and that what was to be most complicated and difficult for them was only just beginning.

Archibald MacLeish

The Old Grey Couple (2)

SHE: Love, says the poet, has no reasons.
HE: Not even after fifty years?
SHE: Particularly after fifty years.
HE: What was it, then, that lured us, that still teases?
SHE: You used to say my plaited hair!
HE: And then you'd laugh.
SHE: Because it wasn't plaited.
Love had no reasons so you made one up
to laugh at. Look! The old, gray couple!

HE: No, to prove the adage true:
Love has no reasons but old lovers do.

SHE: And they can't tell.

HE: I can and so can you.
Fifty years ago we drew each other,
magnetized needle toward the longing north.
It was your naked presence that so moved me.
It was your absolute presence that was love.

SHE: Ah, *was!*

HE: And now, years older, we begin to see
absence not presence: what the world would be
without your footstep in the world—the garden
empty of the radiance where you are.

SHE: And that's your reason?—that old lovers see
their love because they know now what its loss
will be?

HE: Because, like Cleopatra in the play,
they know there's nothing left once love's away . . .

SHE: Nothing remarkable beneath the visiting moon . . .

HE: Ours is the late, last wisdom of the afternoon.
We know that love, like light, grows dearer toward
the dark.

Edna O'Brien

Mrs. Reinhardt

Mrs. Reinhardt had her routes worked out. Blue ink for the main roads, red when she would want to turn off. A system, and a vow. She must enjoy herself, she must rest, she must recuperate, she must put on weight, and perhaps blossom the merest bit. She must get over it. After all, the world was a green, a sunny, an enchanting place. The hay was being gathered, the spotted cows so sleek they looked like Dalmatians and their movements so lazy in the meadows that they could be somnambulists. The men and women working the fields seemed to be devoid of fret or haste. It was June in Brittany, just before the throngs of visitors arrived, and the roads were relatively clear. The weather was blustery, but as she drove along, the occasional patches of sunlight illumined the trees, the lush grass, and the marshes. Seeds and pollen on the surface of the marshes were a bright mustard yellow. Bits of flowering broom divided the roadside, and at intervals an emergency telephone kiosk in bright orange caught her attention. She did not like that. She did not like emergency and she did not like the telephone. To be avoided.

While driving, Mrs. Reinhardt was occupied and her heart was relatively serene. One would not know that recently she had been through so much and that presently much more was to follow. A lull. Observe the roadside, the daisies in the fields, the red and the pink poppies, and the lupins so dozy like the cows; observe the road signs and think in sympathy of the English dead in the last war whose specters floated somewhere in these environments, the English dead of whom some photograph, some relic, or some crushed thought was felt at that moment in some English semidetached home. Think of food, think of shellfish, think of the French or blueberries, think of anything, so long as the mind keeps itself occupied.

It promised to be a beautiful hotel. She had seen photos of it, a dovecote on the edge of a lake, the very essence of stillness, beauty, sequesteredness. A place to remeet the god of peace. On either side of the road the pines were young and spindly, but the cows were pendulous, their udders shockingly large and full. It occurred to her that it was still morning and that they had been only recently milked, so what would they feel like at sundown! What a nuisance that it was those cows' udders that brought the forbidden thought to her mind.

Once, in their country cottage, a cow had got caught in the barbed-wire fence and both she and Mr. Reinhardt had a time of it trying to get help, and then trying to release the creature, causing a commotion among the cow community. Afterward they had drunk champagne, intending to celebrate something. Or was it to hide something? Mr. Reinhardt had said that they must not grow apart and yet had quarreled with her about the Common Market and removed her glasses while she was reading a story by Flaubert sitting up in bed. The beginning of the end, as she now knew, as she then new, or did she, or do we, or is there such a thing, or is it another beginning to another ending, and on and on.

"Damnation," Mrs. Reinhardt said, and speeded just as she came to where there were a variety of signs with thick arrows and names in navy blue. She had lost her bearings. She took a right and realized at once that she had gone to the east town rather than the main town. So much for distraction. Let him go. The worst was already over. She could see the town cathedral as she glanced behind, and already was looking for a way in which to turn right.

The worst was over, the worst being when the other woman, the girl really, was allowed to wear Mrs. Reinhardt's nightdress and necklace. For fun. "She is young," he had said. It seemed she was, this rival, or rather, this replacement. So young that she shouted out of car windows at other motorists, that she carried a big bright umbrella, that she ate chips or cough lozenges on the way to one of these expensive restaurants where Mr. Reinhardt took her. All in all, she was a gamine.

Mrs. Reinhardt drove around a walled city and swore at a system of signs that did not carry the name of the mill town she was looking for. There were other things, like a clock and a bakery and a few strollers, and when she pulled into the tree-lined square, there was a young man naked to the waist in front of an easel, obviously sketching the cathedral. She spread the map over her knees and opened the door to get a puff of air. He looked at her. She smiled at him. She had to smile at someone. All of a sudden she had an irrational wish to have a son, a son who was with her now, to comfort her, to give her confidence, to take her part. Of course, she had a son, but he was grown up and had gone to America and knew none of this and must not know any of this.

THE MAN told her that she need never have gone into the cathedral town, but as she said herself, she had seen it, she had seen the young man painting, she had given a little smile and he had smiled back and that was something. For the rest of the journey she remained alert, she saw trees, gabled houses, a few windmills, she saw dandelions, she passed little towns, she saw washing on the line, and she knew that she was going in the right direction.

HER ARRIVAL was tended with magic. Trees, the sound of running water, flowers, wildflowers, and a sense of being in a place that it would take time to know, take time to discover. To make it even more mysterious, the apartments were stone chalets scattered at a distance throughout the grounds. It was a complex, really, but one in which nature dominated. She went down some steps to where it said RECEPTION and, having introduced herself, was asked at once to hurry so as to be served lunch. Finding the dining room was an expedition in itself—up steps, down more steps, and then into a little outer salon where there were round tables covered with lace cloths and on each table a vase of wildflowers. She bent down and smelled some pansies. A pure sweet silken smell, with the texture of childhood. She felt grateful. Her husband was paying for all this, and what a pity that like her he was not now going down more steps, past a satin screen, to a table laid for two by an open window, to the accompaniment of running water. She had a half bottle of champagne, duck pâté, and a flat white grilled fish on a bed of thin strips of boiled leek. The hollandaise sauce was perfect and yellower than usual because they had added mustard. She was alone except for the serving girl and an older couple at a table a few yards away. She could not hear what they said. The man was drinking Calvados. The serving girl had a pretty face and brown curly hair tied back with a ribbon. One curl had been brought onto her forehead for effect. She radiated innocence and a dream. Mrs. Reinhardt could not avoid looking at her for long and thought, She has probably never been to Paris, never even been to Nantes, but she hopes to go and will go one day. That story was in her eyes, in the curls of her hair, in everything she did. That thirst.

After lunch Mrs. Reinhardt was escorted to her room. It was down a dusty road with ferns and dock on either side. Wild roses of the palest pink tumbled over the arch of the door, and when she stood in her bedroom and looked through one of the narrow turret windows, it was these roses and grassland that she saw, while from the other side she could hear the rush of the water; the two images reminded her of herself and of everybody else that she had known. One was green and hushed and quiet and the other was torrential. Did they have to conflict with each other? She undressed, she unpacked, she opened the little refrigerator to see what delights were there. There was beer and champagne and miniatures of whiskey and Vichy water and red cordial. It was like being a child again and looking into one's little toy house. She had a little weep. For what did Mrs. Reinhardt weep—for beauty, for ugliness, for herself, for her son in America, for Mr. Reinhardt, who had lost his reason. So badly did Mr. Reinhardt love this new girl, Rita, that he had made her take him to meet all her friends so that he could ask them how Rita looked at sixteen, and seventeen, what Rita wore, what Rita was like as a debutante, and why Rita stopped going to art school, and had made notes of these things. Had made an utter fool of himself. Yes, she cried for that, and as she cried, it seemed to her the tears were like the strata of this earth, had many levels and many layers, and that those layers differed, and that now she was crying for more than one thing at the same time, that her tears were all mixed up. She was also crying about age, about two gray ribs in her pubic hair, crying for not having tried harder on certain occasions, as when Mr. Reinhardt came home expecting excitement or repose and getting instead a typical story about the nonarrival of the gas man. She had let herself be drawn into the weary and hypnotizing whirl of domesticity. With her the magazines had to be neat, the dust had to be dusted, all her perfectionism had got thrown into that instead of something larger, or instead of Mr. Reinhardt. Where do we go wrong? Is that not what guardian angels are meant to do, to lead us back by the hand?

She cried, too, because of the night she had thrown a platter at him, and he sat there mortified, and said that he knew he was wrecking her life and his, but that he could not stop it, said maybe it was madness or the male menopause or anything she wanted to call it, but that it was what it was, what it was. He had even appealed to her. He told her a story, he told her that very day when he had gone to an auction to buy some pictures for the gallery, he had brought Rita with him, and as they drove along the motorway, he had hoped that they would crash, so terrible for him was his predicament and so impossible for him was it to be parted from this girl, who he admitted had made him delirious, but Happy, but Happy, as he kept insisting.

It was this helplessness of human beings that made her cry most of all, and when long after, which is to say at sunset, Mrs. Reinhardt had dried her eyes and had put on her oyster dress and her Chinese necklace, she was still repeating to herself this matter of helplessness. At the same time she was reminding herself that there lay ahead a life, adventure, that she had not finished; she had merely changed direction and the new road was unknown to her.

SHE SAT down to dinner. She was at a different table. This time she looked out on a lake that was a tableau of prettiness—trees on either side, overhanging branches, green leaves with silver undersides, and a fallen bough where ducks perched. The residents were mostly elderly, except for one woman with orange hair and studded sunglasses. This woman scanned a magazine throughout the dinner and did not address a word to her escort.

Mrs. Reinhardt would look at the view, have a sip of wine, chew a crust of the bread that was so aerated it was like a communion wafer. Suddenly she looked to one side and there in a tank with bubbles of water within were several lobsters. They were so beautiful that at first she thought they were mannequin lobsters, ornaments. Their shells had beautiful blue tints, the blue of lapis lazuli, and though their movements had at first unnerved her, she began to engross herself in their motion and to forget what was going on around her. They moved beautifully and to such purpose. They moved to touch each other, at least some did, and others waited, were the recipients, so to speak, of this reach, this touch. Their movements had all the grandeur of speech without the folly. But there was no mistaking their intention. So caught up was she in this that she did not hear the pretty girl call her out to the phone, and in fact she had to be touched on the bare arm, which of course made her jump. Naturally she went out somewhat flustered, missed her step, and turned but did not wrench her ankle. It was her weak ankle, the one she always fell on. Going into the little booth, she mettled herself. Perhaps he was contrite or drunk, or else there had been an accident, or else their son was getting married. At any rate, it was crucial. She said her hello calmly but pertly. She repeated it. It was a strange voice altogether, a man asking for Rachel. She said who is Rachel. There were a few moments of heated irritation and then complete disappointment as Mrs. Reinhardt made her way back to her table trembling. Stupid girl to have called her! Only the lobsters saved the occasion.

Now she gave them her full attention. Now she forgot the mistake of the phone and observed the drama that was going on. A great long lobster seemed to be lord of the tank. His claws were covered with black elastic bands, but that did not prevent him from proudly stalking through the water, having frontal battles with some, but chiefly trying to arouse another: a sleeping lobster who was obviously his heart's desire. His appeals to her were mesmerizing. He would tickle her with his antennae, he would put claws over her, then edge a claw under her so that he levered her up a fraction, and then he would leave her be for an instant, only to return with a stronger, with a more telling, assault. Of course there were moments when he had to desist, to ward off others who were coming in her region, and this he did with the same determination, facing them with eyes that were vicious yet immobile as beads. He would lunge through the water and drive them back or drive them elsewhere, and then he would return as if to his love and to his oracle. There were secondary movements in the tank, of course, but it was at the main drama Mrs. Reinhardt looked. She presumed it was a him and gave him the name of Napoleon. At times so great was his sexual plight that he would lower a long antenna under his rear and touch the little dun bibs of membrane and obviously excite himself so that he could start afresh on his sleeping lady. Because he was in no doubt but that she would succumb. Mrs. Reinhardt christened her the Japanese Lady, because of her languor, her refusal to be roused, by him, or by any of them, and Mrs. Reinhardt thought, Oh, what a sight it will be when she does rise up and give herself to his embraces; oh, what a wedding that will be! Mrs. Reinhardt also thought that it was very likely that they would only be in this tank for a short number of hours and that in those hours they must act the play of their lives. Looking at them, with her hands pressed together, she hoped, the way children hope, for a happy ending to this courtship.

She had to leave the dining room while it was still going on, but in some way, she felt, with the lights out and visitors gone, the protagonists, safe in their tank, secured by air bubbles, secretly would find each other. She had drunk a little too much, and she swayed slightly as she went down the dusty road to her chalet. She felt elated. She had seen something that moved her. She had seen instinct, she had seen the grope, and she had seen the will that refuses to be refused. She had seen tenderness.

In her bedroom she put the necklace into the heart-shaped wicker box and hid it under the bolster of the second bed. She had robbed her husband of it—this beautiful choker of jade. It had been his mother's. It was worth ten thousand pounds. It was her going-away present. She had extracted it from him. Before closing it in the box she bit on the beads as if they were fruit.

"If you give me the necklace I will go away." That was what she had said, and she knew that in some corner she was thereby murdering his heart. It was his family necklace and it was the one thing in which he believed his luck was invested. Also, he was born under the sign of Cancer and if he clung, he clung. It was the thing they shared, and by taking it she was telling him that she was going away forever, and that she was taking some of him, his most important talisman, relic of his mother, relic of their life together. She had now become so involved with this piece of jewelry that when she wore it she touched her throat constantly to make sure that it was there, and when she took it off, she kissed it, and at night she dreamed of it, and one night she dreamed that she had tucked it into her vagina for safety and hidden it there. At other times she thought how she would go to the casino and gamble it away, his luck and hers. There was a casino nearby and on Saturday there was to be a cycling tournament, and she thought that one night, maybe on Saturday, she would go out, and maybe she would gamble and maybe she would win. Soon she fell asleep.

On the third day Mrs. Reinhardt went driving. She needed a change of scene. She needed sea air and crag. She needed invigoration. The little nest was cloying. The quack-quack of the ducks, the running water were all very well, but they were beginning to echo her own cravings and she did not like that. So after breakfast she read the seventeenth-century Nun's Prayer, the one which asked the Lord to release one from excessive speech, to make one thoughtful but not moody, to give one a few friends and to keep one reasonably sweet. She thought of Rita. Rita's bright blue eyes, sapphire eyes, and the little studs in her ears that matched. Rita was ungainly, like a colt. Rita would be the kind of girl who could stay up all night, swim at dawn, and then sleep like a baby all through the day, even in an unshaded room. Youth. Yet it so happened that Mrs. Reinhardt had found an admirer. The Monsieur who owned the hotel had paid her more than passing attention. In fact, she hardly had to turn a corner but he was there, and he could find some distraction to delay her for a moment, so as he could gaze upon her. First it was a hare running through the undergrowth, then it was his dog following some ducks, then it was the electricity van coming to mend the telephone cable. The dreaded telephone. She was pleased that it was out of order. She was also pleased that she was still striking, and there was no denying but that Mrs. Reinhardt could bewitch people.

It was when judging a young persons' art exhibition that he met Rita. Rita's work was the worst, and realizing this, she had torn it up in a tantrum. He came home and told Mrs. Reinhardt and said how sorry he had felt for her but how plucky she had been. It was February the twenty-second. The following day two things happened—he bought several silk shirts and he proposed they go to Paris for a weekend.

"If only I could turn the key on it and close the door and come back when I am an old woman, if only I could do that." So Mrs. Reinhardt said to herself as she drove away from the green nest, from the singing birds and the hovering midges, from the rich hollandaise sauces and the quilted bed, from the overwhelming comfort of it all. Indeed, she thought she might have suffocated her husband in the very same way. For though Mrs. Reinhardt was cold to others, distant in her relationships with men and women, this was not her true nature; this was something she had built up, a screen of reserve to shelter her fear. She was sentimental at home and used to do a million things for Mr. Reinhardt to please him, and to pander to him. She used to warm his side of the bed while he was still undressing, or looking at a drawing he had just bought, or even pacing the room. The pacing had grown more acute. When she knit his socks in cable stitch she always knit a third sock in case one got torn or ruined. While he was fishing or when he hunted in Scotland in August, she went just to be near him, though she dreaded these forays. They were too public. House parties of people thrown in upon each other for a hectic and sociable week. There was no privacy. Some of the women would go as beaters, while some would sit in one of the drawing rooms swapping recipes or discussing face-lifts, good clothes, or domestic service bureaus. The landscape and the grouse were the same wonderful color—that of rusted metal. The shot birds often seemed as if they had just lain down in jest, so undead did they seem. Even the few drops of blood seemed unreal, theatrical. She loved the moors, the rusted color of farm and brushwood. She loved the dogs and the excitement, but she balked at the sound of the shots. A sudden violence in those untouched moors and then the glee as the hunters went in search of their kill. He might wink at her once or pass her a cup of bouillon when they sat down, but he didn't include her in conversation. He didn't have to. She often thought that the real secret of their love was that she kept the inside of herself permanently warm for him, like someone keeping an egg under a nest of straw. When she loved, she loved completely, rather like a spaniel. Her eyes were the same yellow-brown. As a young girl she was using a sewing machine one day and by accident put the needle through her index finger, but she did not call out to her parents, who were in the other room, she waited until her mother came through. Upon seeing this casualty her mother let out a scream. Within an instant her father was by her side, and with a jerk of the lever he lifted the thing out and gave her such a look, such a loving look. Mrs. Reinhardt was merely Tilly then, an only daughter, and full of trust. She believed that you loved your mother and father, that you loved your brother, that eventually you loved your husband, and then, most of all, that you loved your children. Her parents had spoiled her, had brought her to the Ritz for birthdays, had left gold trinkets on her pillow on Christmas Eve, had comforted her when she wept. When she was twenty-one, they had an expensive portrait done of her and hung it on the wall in a prominent position so that as guests entered they would say, "Who is that! Who is that!" and a rash of compliments would follow.

When she turned thirty, her husband had her portrait painted; it was in their sitting room at that very moment, watching him and Rita, unless he had turned it around, or unless Rita had splashed house paint over it. Rita was unruly, it seemed. Rita's jealousy was more drastic than the occasional submarines of jealousy Mrs. Reinhardt had experienced in their seventeen years of marriage—then it was over women roughly her own age, women with poise, women with husbands, women with guile, women who made a career of straying but were back in their homes by six o'clock. Being jealous of Rita was a more abstract thing—they had met only once and that was on the steps of a theater. Rita had followed him there, run up the steps, handed him a note, and run off again. Being jealous of Rita was being jealous of youth, of freedom, and of spontaneity. Rita did not want marriage or an engagement ring. She wanted to go to Florence, she wanted to go to a ball, to go to the park on roller skates. Rita had a temper. Once at one of her father's soirées she threw twenty gold chairs out the window. If they had had a daughter, things might now be different. And if their son lived at home, things might now be different. Four people might have sat down at a white table, under a red umbrella, looked out at a brown lake, whose color was dimmed by the cluster of trees and saplings. There might be four glasses, one with Coca-Cola, one or maybe two with whiskey, and hers with white wine and soda water. A young voice might say, "What is that?" pointing to a misshapen straw basket on a wooden plinth in the middle of the lake, and as she turned her attention to discern what it was, and as she decided that it was a nest for either swans or ducks, the question would be repeated with a touch of impatience—"Mam, what is that?" and Mrs. Reinhardt might be answering. Oh my, yes, the family tableau smote her.

So transported back was she, to the hotel and a united family, that Mrs. Reinhardt was like a sleepwalker traversing the rocks that were covered with moss and then the wet sand between the rocks. She was making her way toward the distant crags. On the sand there lay caps of seaweed so green, and so shaped like the back of a head, that they were like theatrical wigs. She looked down at one, she bent to pore over its greenness, and when she looked up, he was there. A man in his mid-twenties in a blue shirt with lips parted seemed to be saying something pleasant to her, though perhaps it was only hello, or hi there. He had an American accent. Had they met in a cocktail bar or at an airport lounge, it is doubtful that they would have spoken, but here the situation called for it. One or the other had to express or confirm admiration for the sea, the boats, the white houses on the far side, the whiteness of the light, the vista; and then quite spontaneously he had to grip her wrist and said, "Look, look," as a bird dived down into the water, swooped up again, redived until he came up with a fish.

"A predator," Mrs. Reinhardt said, his hand still on her wrist, casually. They argued about the bird; she said it was a gannet and he said it was some sort of hawk. She said sweetly that she knew more about wildlife than he did. He conceded. He said if you came from Main Street, Iowa, you knew nothing, you were a hick. They laughed.

As they walked back along the shore, he told her how he had been staying farther up with friends and had decided to move on because one never discovers anything except when alone. He'd spend a night or two and then move on, and eventually he would get to Turkey. He wasn't doing a grand tour or a gastronomic tour, he was just seeing the wild parts of Brittany and had found a hotel on the other side that was hidden from everybody. "The savage side," he said.

By the time she had agreed to have a crêpe with him, they had exchanged those standard bits of information. He confessed that he didn't speak much French. She confessed that she'd taken a crammer course and was even thinking of spending three months in Paris to do a cookery course. When they went indoors she removed her headscarf and he was caught at once by the beauty of her brown pile of hair. Some hidden urge of vanity made her toss it as they looked for a table.

"Tell me something," he said, "are you married or not?"

"Yes and no . . ." She had removed her wedding ring and put it in the small leather box that snapped when one shut it.

He found her reply intriguing. Quickly she explained that she had been but was about not to be. He reached out but did not touch her, and she thought that there was something exquisite in that, that delicate indication of sympathy. He said quietly how he had missed out on marriage and on kids. She felt that he meant it. He said he had been a wildcat, and whenever he had met a nice girl he had cheated on her and lost her. He could never settle down.

"I'm bad news," he said, and laughed, and there was something so impish about him that Mrs. Reinhardt was being won over.

On closer acquaintance she had to admit that his looks were indeed flawless. So perhaps his character was not as terrible as he had made out. She pressed him to tell her things, boyish things like his first holiday in Greece, or his first girl, or his first guitar, and gradually she realized she was becoming interested in these things although in them there was nothing new. It was the warmth really and the way he delighted in telling her these things that made Mrs.

Reinhardt ask for more stories. She was like someone who has been on a voyage and upon return wants to hear everything that has happened on land. He told her that he had made a short film that he would love her to see. He would fly home for it that night if only he could! It was a film about motorcycling and he had made it long before anyone else had made a film about it, or written a book about it. He told her some of the stories. Scenes at dusk in a deserted place when a man gets a puncture and says, "What the hell does it matter . . ." as he sits down to take a smoke. She sensed a purity in him alongside everything else. He loved the desert, he loved the prairie, but yes, he had lived on women and he had drunk a lot and he had slept rough and he had smoked every kind of weed under the sun, and he wished he had known Aldous Huxley, that Aldous Huxley had been his dad.

"Still searching," he said.

"It's the fashion now," she said a little dryly.

"Hey, let's get married," he said, and they clapped hands and both pretended it was for real. Both acted a little play; it was the same as if someone had come into the room and said, "Do it for real, kids." In jest, their cheeks met; in jest, their fingers interlocked; in jest, their knuckles mashed one another's; and in jest, they stood up, moved onto the small dance area, and danced as closely as Siamese twins might to the music from the jukebox. In jest, or perhaps not, Mrs. Reinhardt felt through the beautiful folds of her oyster dress the press of his sexuality, and round and round and round they danced, the two jesting betrothed people, who were far from home and who had got each other into such a spin of excitement. How thrilling it was and how rejuvenating to dance round and round and feel the strength and the need of this man pushing closer and closer to her while still keeping her reserve. On her face the most beautiful ecstatic smile. She was smiling for herself. He did slide his other hand on her buttock, but Mrs. Reinhardt just shrugged it off. The moment the dancing stopped they parted.

Soon after they sat down, she looked at her tiny wristwatch, peered at it, and at once he flicked on his blue plastic lighter so that she could read the tiny black insectlike hands. Then he held the lighter in front of her face to admire her, to admire the eyes, the long nose, the sensual mouth, the necklace.

"Real," he said, picking up the green beads that she herself had become so involved with and had been so intimate with.

"Think so," she said, and regretted it instantly. After all, the world did abound in thieves and rogues, and ten thousand pounds was no joke to be carrying around. She had read of women such as she, who took up with men, younger men or older men, only to be robbed, stripped of their possessions, bled. She curdled within and suddenly invented for herself a telephone call back at the hotel. When she excused herself, he rose chivalrously, escorted her through the door, down the steps, and across the gravel path to the car park. They did not kiss good night.

IN THE MORNING the world was clean and bright. There had been rain and everything got washed, the water mills, the ducks, the roses, the trees, the lupins, and the little winding paths. The little winding paths, of course, were strewn with white, pink, and pale blue blossoms. The effect was as of seeing snow when she opened the windows, leaned out, and broke a rose that was still damp and whose full smell had not been restored yet. Its smell was smothered by the smell of rain, and that, too, was beautiful. And so were her bare breasts resting on the window ledge. And so was life, physical well-being, one's own body, roses, encounter, promise, the dance. She drew back quickly when she saw that there Monsieur was, down below, idly hammering a few nails into a wall. He seemed to be doing this to make a trellis for the roses, but he was in no hurry as he looked in her direction. He had a knack of finding her no matter where she was. The night before, as she drove back late, he was in the car park to say that they had kept her a table for dinner. He had brought a spare menu in his pocket. The big black dog looked up, too. Somehow her own whiteness and the milklikeness of her breasts contrasted with the blackness of the dog, and she saw them detached, yet grouped together in a very beautiful painting, opposites, one that was long and black with a snout, and one that was white and like the globe of a lamp. She liked that picture and would add it to the pictures that she had seen during the years she sleepwalked. She sleepwalked no longer. Life was like that, you dreamed a lot, or you cried a lot, or you itched a lot, and then it disappeared and something else came in its place.

Mrs. Reinhardt dawdled. She put on one dress, then another; she lifted a plate ashtray and found a swarm of little ants underneath; she took sparkling mineral water from the refrigerator, drank it, took two of her iron tablets, and by a process of association pulled her lower eyelid down to see if she was still anemic. She realized something wonderful. For whatever number of minutes it had been, she had not given a thought to Mr. Reinhardt, and this was the beginning of recovery. That was how it happened, one forgot for two minutes and remembered for twenty. One forgot for three minutes and remembered for fifteen, but as with a pendulum the states of remembering and the states of forgetting were gradually equalized, and then one great day the pendulum had gone over and the states of forgetting had gained a victory. What more did a woman want? Mrs. Reinhardt danced around the room, leaped over her bed, threw a pillow in the air, and felt as alive and gay as the day she got engaged and knew she would live happily ever after. What more did a woman want? She wanted this American, although he might be a bounder. He might not. She would have him, but in her own time and to suit her own requirements. She would not let him move into her hotel apartment because the privacy of it was sacred. In fact, she was beginning to enjoy herself. Think of it, she could have coffee at noon instead of nine-thirty, she could eat an éclair, she could pluck her eyebrows, she could sing high notes and low notes, she could wander.

"Freedom!" Mrs. Reinhardt told the lovely supple woman in the flowered dressing gown who smiled into the long mirror while the other Mrs. Reinhardt told the lovely woman that the mirabelle she had drunk the night before was still swishing through her brain.

After breakfast she walked in the woods. Crossing a little plaited bridge, she took off her sandals and tiptoed so as not to disturb the sounds and activities of nature. It was the darkest wood she had ever entered. All the trees twined overhead, so that it was a vault with layer upon layer of green. Ferns grew in wizard abundance, and between the ferns other things strove to be seen, while all about were the butterflies and the insects. Mushrooms and toadstools flourished at the base of every tree, and she knelt down to smell them. She loved their dank smell. The air was pierced with birdsong of every note and every variety as the birds darted across the ground or swooped up into the air. This fecundity of nature, this chorus of birds and the distant cooing of the doves from the dovecote, thrilled her and presently something else quickened her desires. The low, suggestive, all-desiring whistle of a male reached her ears. She had almost walked over him. He could see her bare legs under her dress. She drew back. He was lying down with his shirt open. He did not rise to greet her.

"You," she said.

He put up his foot in salutation. She stood over him, trying to decide whether his presence was welcome or an intrusion.

"Amazing," he said, and held his hands out, acceding to the abundance of nature about him. He apologized for his presence but said that he had cycled over to see her just to say hello, he had brought her some croissants hot from the oven, but upon hearing she was sleeping, he decided to have a ramble in the woods. He had fed the croissants to the birds. He used some French words to impress her and she laughed and soon her petulance was washed away. After all, they were not her woods, and he had not knocked on her bedroom door, and she would have been disappointed if he had cycled off without seeing her. She spread her dress like a cushion underneath her and sat, folding her legs to the other side. It was then they talked. They talked for a long time. They talked of courage, the different courage of men and women. The courage when a horse bolts or the car in front of one crashes, the draining courage of everyday. She said men were never able to say *"finito."* "Damn right," he said, and the jargon struck her as comic compared with the peace and majesty of the woods.

"You smell good," he would sometimes say, and that, too, belonged to another environment, but for the most part he impressed her with his sincerity and with the way he took his time to say the thing he wanted to say. Before the week was out she would lead him to her bed. It would be stark and it would be unexpected, an invitation tossed at the very last minute, as when someone takes a flower or a handkerchief, and throws it into the bullring. She would be unabashed, as she had not been for years. They stayed for about an hour, talking, and at times one or the other would get up, walk or run toward the little bridge, and pretend to take a photograph. Eventually they got up together and went to find his bicycle. He insisted that she cycle. After the first few wobbles she rode down the path and could hear him clapping. Then she got off, turned around, and rode back toward him. He said that next time she would have to stay on the bicycle while turning around, and she biffed him and said she had not ridden for years. Her face was flushed and bicycle oil had got on her skirt. For fun he sat her on the bar of the bicycle, put his leg across, and they set off down the avenue at a dizzying speed, singing, "Daisy, Daisy, give me your answer, do. I'm half crazy, all for the love of you . . ."

He would not stop, even though she swore that she was going to fall off any minute.

"You're O.K. . . ." he'd say as he turned the next corner. In a while she stopped screaming and enjoyed the queasiness in her stomach.

MRS. REINHARDT stood in the narrow shower, the disk of green soap held under one armpit, when she saw a rose branch being waved into the room. As in a mirage the petals randomly fell. Which of them was it? Him or Monsieur? She was feeling decidedly amorous. He climbed in through the window and came directly to her. He did not speak. He gripped her roughly, his own clothing still on, and he was so busy taking possession of her that he did not realize that he was getting drenched. The shower was full on, yet neither of them bothered to turn it off. The zipper of his trousers hurt her, but he was mindless of that. The thing is, he had desired her from the very first, and now he was pumping all his arrogance and all his cockatooing into her and she was taking it gladly, also gluttonously. She was recovering her pride as a woman, and much more, as a desirable woman. It was this she had sorely missed in the last ten months. Yet she was surprised by herself, surprised by her savage need to get even with life, or was it to get healed? She leaned against the shower wall, wet and slippery all over, and lolled so that every bit of her was partaking of him. She did not worry about him, though he did seem in quite a frenzy both to prove himself and to please her, and he kept uttering the vilest of words, calling her sow and dog and bitch, and so forth. She even thought that she might conceive, so radical was it, and the only other thought that came to her was of the lobsters and the lady lobster lying so still while all the others sought her.

When he came, she refused to claim to be satisfied and with a few rough strokes insisted he fill her again and search for her every crevice. This all happened without speech except for the names he muttered as she squeezed from him the juices he did not have left to give. She was certainly getting her own back.

Afterward she washed, and as he lay on the bathroom floor out of breath, she stepped over him and went to her room to rest. She felt like a queen, and lying on her bed, her whole body was like a ship decked out with beauty. A victory! She had locked the bedroom door. Let him wait, let him sweat. She would join him for dinner. She had told him so in French, knowing it would doubly confound him. She went to sleep, ordering herself pleasant dreams, colored dreams, the colors of sunlight and of lightning, yellow sun and saffron lightning.

HE KEPT the dinner appointment. Mrs. Reinhardt saw him from a landing, down in the little salon, where there were lace-covered tables and vases of wildflowers. She remembered it from her first day. He was drinking a Pernod. It was almost dark down there except for the light from the table candles. It was a somewhat somber place. The drawings on the wall were all of monks or ascetics, and nailed to a cross of wood was a bird; it seemed to be a dead pheasant. He was wearing green, a green silk dinner jacket—had she not seen it somewhere? Yes, it had been on display in the little hotel showcase where they also sold jewelry and beachwear.

The moment she went to his table she perceived the change in him. The good-natured truant boy had given way to the slightly testy seducer, and he did not move a chair or a muscle as she sat down. He called to Michele, the girl with the curly hair, to bring another Pernod, in fact, to bring two. Mrs. Reinhardt thought that it was just a ruse and that he was proving to her what a man of the world he was. She said she had slept well.

"Where's your loot?" he said, looking at her neck. She had left it in her room and was wearing pearls instead. She did not answer but merely held up the paperback book to show that she had been reading.

"You read that?" he said. It was D. H. Lawrence.

"I haven't read that stuff since I was twelve," he said. He was drunk. It augured badly. She wondered if she should dismiss him there and then, but as on previous occasions when things got very bad, Mrs. Reinhardt became very stupid, became inept. He gave the waitress a wink and gripped her left hand, where she was wearing a bracelet. She moved off as languidly as always.

"You're a doll," he said.

"She doesn't speak English," Mrs. Reinhardt said.

"She speaks my kind of English," he said.

It was thus in a state of anger, pique, and agitation that they went in to dinner. As he studied the four menus, he decided on the costliest one and said it was a damn good thing that she was a rich bitch.

"Rich bitch," he said, and laughed.

She let it pass. He said how about taking him to Pamplona for the bullfights and then went into a rhapsody about past fights and past bullfighters.

"Oh, you read it in Ernest Hemingway," she said, unable to resist a sting.

"Oh, we've got a hot and cold lady," he said as he held the velvet-covered wine list in front of him. The lobster tank was gapingly empty. There were only three lobsters in there and those lay absolutely still. Perhaps they were shocked from the raid and were lying low, not making a stir, so as not to be seen. She was on the verge of tears. He ordered a classic bottle of wine. It meant the girl getting Monsieur, who then had to get his key and go to the cellar and ceremoniously bring it back and show the label and open it and decant it and wait. The waitress had changed clothes because she was going to the cycle tournament. Her black pinafore was changed for a blue dress with colors in the box pleats. She looked enchanting. Ready for showers of kisses and admiration.

"How would you like me to fuck you?" he said to the young girl, who watched the pouring of the wine.

"You have gone too far," Mrs. Reinhardt said, and perhaps fear-ing that she might make a scene, he leaned over to her and said: "Don't worry, I'll handle you."

She excused herself, more for the waitress than for him, and hurried out. Never in all her life had Mrs. Reinhardt been so angry. She sat on the hammock in the garden and asked the stars and the lovely hexagonal lamps and the sleeping ducks to please succor her in this nightmare. She thought of the bill and the jacket, which she realized would also be on her bill, and she cried like a very angry child who is unable to tell anyone what happened. Her disgrace was extreme. She swung back and forth in the hammock, cursing and swearing, then praying for patience. The important thing was never to have to see him again. She was shivering and in a state of shock by the time she went to her room. She really went to put on a cardigan and to order a sandwich or soup. There he was in her dressing gown. He had quit dinner, he said, being as she so rudely walked away. He, too, was about to order a sandwich. The fridge door was open, and as she entered he clicked it closed. Obviously he had drunk different things, and she could see that he was wild. He was not giving this up, this luxury, this laissez-faire. He rose and staggered.

"Round one," he said, and caught her.

"Get out of here," she said.

"Not me, I'm in for the licks."

Mrs. Reinhardt knew with complete conviction that she was about to be the witness of, and a participant in, the most sordid kind of embroilment. Alacrity took hold of her, and she thought, Coax him, seem mature, laugh, divert him. But seeing the craze in his eyes, instinct made her resort to stronger measures, and the scream she let out was astounding even to her own ears. It was no more than seconds until Monsieur was in the room grappling with him. She realized that he had been watching all along and that he had been prepared for this in a way that she was not. Monsieur was telling him in French to get dressed and to get lost. It had some elements of farce.

"O.K., O.K.," he was saying. "Just let me get dressed, just let me get out of this asshole."

She was glad of the language barrier. Then an ugly thing happened; the moment Monsieur let go of him, he used a dirty trick. He picked up the empty champagne bottle and wielded it at his opponent's head. Suddenly the two of them were in a clinch. Mrs. Reinhardt searched her mind for what was best to do. She picked up a chair, but her action was like someone in slow motion, because while they were each forcing each other onto the ground, she was holding the chair and not doing anything with it. It was the breaking bottle she dreaded most of all. By then her hand had been on the emergency bell, and as they both fell to the floor, the assistant chef came in with a knife. He must have dashed from the kitchen. The two men were, of course, able to master the situation, and when he got up, he was shaking his head like a boxer who has been badly punched.

Monsieur suggested that she leave and go over to Reception and wait there. As she left the room, he gave her his jacket. Walking down the little road, her body shook like jelly. The jacket kept slipping off. She was conscious of having just escaped indescribable horror. Horror such as one reads of. She realized how sheltered her life had been, but this was no help. What she really wanted was to sit with someone and talk about anything. The hotel lounge was propriety itself. Another young girl, also with a rose in her hair, was slowly preparing a tray of drinks. A party of Dutch people sat in a corner, the dog snapped at some flies, and from the other room came the strains of music, as there was a wedding in progress. Mrs. Reinhardt sat in a deep leather chair and let all those pleasant things lap over her. She could hear speeches and clapping and then the sweet and lovely strains of the accordion, and though she could not explain to herself why these sounds made her feel enormously safe, made her feel as if perhaps she were getting married, she realized that that was the nice aftermath of shock.

THE PRINCIPAL excitement next morning was the birth of seven baby ducks. The little creatures had been plunged into the brown rushing water while a delighted audience looked on. Other ducks sat curled up on stones, sulking, perhaps since they were so ignored in favor of a proud mother and these little daft naked creatures. The doves, too, fanned their tails in utter annoyance, while everyone looked toward the water and away from them. She sat and sipped coffee. Monsieur sat a little away from her, dividing his admiration between her and the baby ducks. He flaked bread between his hands, then opened the sliding door and pitched it out. Then he would look at her and smile. Speech was beyond him. He had fallen in love with her, or was infatuated, or was pretending to be infatuated. One of these things. Maybe he was just salvaging her pride. Yet the look was genuinely soft, even adoring. His swallow was affected, his cheeks were as red as the red poppies, and he did little things like wind his watch or rearrange the tops of his socks all for her benefit. Once he put his hand on her shoulder to alert her to some new minutiae of the ducks' behavior and he pressed achingly on her flesh.

If Madame were to find out! she thought, and her being shuddered at the prospect of any further unpleasantness. She did not ask about the bounder, but she did ask later for a glance at her bill and there indeed was the *veston*, the gentleman's *veston*, for sixteen hundred francs. After breakfast she sat out on the lawn and observed the behavior of the other ducks. They pass their time very amiably, she thought; they doze a lot, then scratch or clean themselves, then doze again, then have a little waddle, and perhaps stretch themselves, but she doubted that a duck walked more than a furlong throughout its whole life. Then on beautiful crested hotel notepaper she wrote to her son. She deliberately wrote a blithe letter, a letter about ducks, trees, and nature. Two glasses with the sucked crescent of an orange in each one were laid in an alcove in the wall and she described this to him and thought that soon she would be indulgent and order a champagne cocktail. She did not say, "Your father and I have separated." She would say it later when the pain was not quite so acute, and when it did not matter so much. When would that be? Mrs. Reinhardt looked down at the cushion she was sitting on, and saw that it was a hundred percent Fibranne, and as far as she was concerned, that was the only thing in the world she could be absolutely sure of.

Going back to her room before lunch, she decided to put on a georgette dress and her beads. She owed it to Monsieur. She ought to look nice, even if she could not smile. She ought to pretend to, and by pretending she might become that person. All the burning thoughts and all the recent wounds might just lie low in her and she could appear to be as calm and unperturbed as a summer lake with its water-lily leaves and its starry flowers. Beneath the surface the carp that no one would cast down for. Monsieur's tenderness meant a lot to her, it meant she was still a person on whom another person lavished attention, even love.

Poor lobsters, she thought, and remembered those beseeching moves. When she opened the heart-shaped box in which the beads were hidden, Mrs. Reinhardt let out a shriek. Gone. Gone. Her talisman, her life insurance, her last link with her husband, Harold, gone. Their one chance of being reunited. Gone. She ran back the road to Reception. She was wild. Madame was most annoyed at being told that such a valuable thing had been so carelessly left lying around. As for theft, she did not want to hear of such a thing. It was a vulgarity, was for a different kind of premises altogether, not for her beautiful three-star establishment. She ran a perfect premises, which was her pride and joy and which was a bower against the outside world. How dare the outside world come into her province. Monsieur's face dissolved in deeper and deeper shades of red and a most wretched expression. He did not say a word. Madame said, of course, it was the visitor, the American gentleman, and there was no knowing what else he had taken. As far as Madame was concerned, the scum of the earth had come into her nest, and though it was a small movement, it was a telling one, when she picked up a vase of flowers, put them down in another place, and put them down so that the water splashed out of them and stained the account she was preparing. This led to a greater vexation. It was a moment of utter terseness, and poor Monsieur could help neither of them. He pulled the dog's ear. Mrs. Reinhardt must ring her husband. She had to. There in full view of them, while Madame scratched figures onto the page and Monsieur pulled the dog's ear, Mrs. Reinhardt said to her husband, Harold, in England that her beads had been stolen, that his beads had been stolen, that their beads had been stolen, and she began to cry. He was no help at all. He asked if they could be traced and she said she doubted it.

"A case of hit-and-run," she said, hoping he would know what she meant. Perhaps he did, because his next remark was that she seemed to be having an eventful time. She said she was in a bad way, and she prayed to God that he would say, "Come home." He didn't. He said he would get in touch with the insurance people.

"Oh, fuck the insurance people," Mrs. Reinhardt said, and slammed the phone down. Monsieur turned away. She walked out the door. She had not a friend in the world.

Mrs. Reinhardt experienced one of those spells that can unsettle one forever. The world became black. A blackness permeated her heart. It was like rats scraping at her brain. It was pitiless. Phrases such as "how are you," or "I love you," or "dear one" were mockery incarnate. The few faces of the strange people around her assumed the masks of animals. The world she stood up in, and was about to fall down in, was green and pretty, but in a second it would be replaced by a bottomless pit into which Mrs. Reinhardt was about to fall for eternity. She fainted.

They must have attended to her, because when she came to, her court shoes were removed, the buttons of her blouse were undone, and there was a warm cup of *tisane* on a stool beside her. A presence had just vanished. Or a ghost. Had just slipped away. She thought it was a woman, and perhaps it was her mother anointing her with ashes, and she thought it was Ash Wednesday. "Because I do not hope to live again," she then said, but fortunately no one seemed to understand. She sat up, sipped the hot tea, apologized about the necklace and about the scene she had made. She was uncertain how far she had gone. King Lear's touching of the robe of Cordelia sprang to mind and she asked God if the dead could in fact live again; if she could witness the miracle that the three apostles witnessed when they came and saw the stone rolled away from Christ's grave. "Come back," she whispered, and it was as if she were taking her own hand and leading herself back to life. The one that led was her present self and the one that was being led was a small child who loved God, loved her parents, loved the trees and the countryside, and had never wanted anything to change. Her two selves stood in the middle, teetering. These were extreme moments for Mrs. Reinhardt, and had she surrendered to them she would have toppled indeed. She asked for water. The tumbler she was holding went soft beneath her grip, and the frightened child in her felt a memory as of shedding flesh, but the woman in her smiled and assured everyone that the crisis had passed, which indeed it had. She lay back for a while and listened to the running water as it lashed and lashed against the jet-black millstone, and she resolved that by afternoon she would go away and bid goodbye to this episode that had had in it enchantment, revenge, shame, and the tenderness of Monsieur.

AS SHE DROVE away, Monsieur came from behind the tree house bearing a small bunch of fresh pansies. They were multicolored, but the two predominant colors were yellow and maroon. They smelled like young skin and had that same delicacy. Mrs. Reinhardt thanked him and cherished the moment. It was like an assuage. She smiled into his face, their eyes met; for him, too, it was a moment of real happiness, fleeting but real, a moment of good.

The new hotel was on a harbor, and for the second time in four days she walked over boulders that were caked with moss. At her feet the bright crops of seaweed that again looked like theater wigs, but this time she saw who was before and behind her. She was fully in control. What maddened her was that women did as she did all the time and that their pride was not stripped from them, nor their jewelry. Or perhaps they kept it a secret. One had to be so cunning, so concealed.

Looking out along the bay at the boats, the masts, and the occasional double sails, she realized that now indeed her new life had begun, a life of adjustment and change. Life with a question mark. Your ideal of human life is? she asked herself. The answer was none.

It had always been her husband, their relationship, his art gallery, their cottage in the country, and plans. One thing above all others came to her mind; it was the thousands of flower petals under the hall carpet which she had put there for pressing. Those pressed flowers were the moments of their life, and what would happen to them—they would lie there for years, or else they would be swept away. She could see them there, thousands of sweet bright petals, mementos of their hours. Before her walk she had been reading Ruskin, reading of the necessary connection between beauty and morality, but it had not touched her. She wanted someone to love. As far as she was concerned, Ruskin's theories were fine sermons, but that is not what the heart wants. She must go home soon and get a job. She must try. Mrs. Reinhardt ran, got out of breath, stood to look at the harbor, ran again, and by an effort of will managed to extricate herself from the rather melancholy state she was in.

During dinner the headwaiter came, between each of the beautiful courses, and asked how she liked them. One was a fish terrine, its colors summery white, pink, green, the colors of flowers. She would love to learn how to make it. Then she had dressed crab, and even the broken-off claws had been dusted with flour and baked for a moment, so that the effect was the same as of smelling warm bread. Everything was right and everything was bright. The little potted plant on the table was a bright cherry pink, robins darted in and out of the dark trees, and the ornamental plates in a glass cupboard had patterns of flowers and trelliswork.

"A gentleman to see you," the younger waiter said. Mrs. Reinhardt froze: the bounder was back. Like a woman ready for battle, she put down her squashed napkin and stalked out of the room. She had to turn a corner to enter the main hall, and there sitting on one of the high-backed Spanish-type chairs was her husband, Mr. Reinhardt. He stood up at once and they shook hands formally, like an attorney and his client at an auspicious meeting. He has come to sue me, she thought, because of the necklace. She did not say, "Why have you come?" He looked tired. Mrs. Reinhardt flinched when she heard that he had taken a private plane. He had been to the other hotel and had motored over. He refused a drink and would not look at her. He was mulling over his attack. She was convinced that she was about to be shot when he put his hand in his pocket and drew the thing out. She did not mind being shot but thought irrationally of the mess on the beautiful Spanish furniture.

"They found it," he said, as he produced the necklace and laid it on the table between them. It lay like a snake in a painting, coiled in order to spring. Yet the sight of it filled her with tears, and she blubbered out about the bounder and how she had met him and how he had used her, and suddenly she realized that she was telling him something that he had no inkling of.

"The maid took them," he said, and she saw the little maid with the brown curly hair dressed for the tournament, and now she could have plucked her tongue out for having precipitated the tale of the bounder.

"Was she sacked?" she asked.

He did not know. He thought not.

"Fine place they have," he said, referring to the lake and the windmills.

"This also is lovely," she said, and went on to talk about the view from the dining room and the light which was so telling, so white, so unavoidable. Just like their predicament. In a minute he would get up and go. If only she had not told him about the bounder. If only she had let him say why he had come. She had closed the last door.

"How have you been?" he said.

"Well," she said, but the nerve in her lower jaw would not keep still, and without intending it and without in any way wanting it to happen, Mrs. Reinhardt burst into tears, much to the astonishment of the young waiter, who was waiting to take an order, as he thought, for a drink.

"He tried to blackmail me," she said, and then immediately denied it.

Her husband was looking at her very quietly, and she was not sure if there was any sympathy left in him. She thought, If he walks out now, it will be catastrophic, and again she thought of the few lobsters who were left in the tank, and who were motionless with grief.

"There is us and there are people like him," Mr. Reinhardt said, and though she had not told the whole story, he sensed the gravity of it. He said that if she did not mind he would stay, and that since he was hungry and since it was late, might they not go in to dinner. She looked at him and her eyes were probably drenched.

"Us and people like him!" she said.

Mr. Reinhardt nodded.

"And Rita?" Mrs. Reinhardt said.

He waited. He looked about. He was by no means at ease.

"She is one of us," he said, and then qualified it. "Or she could be, if she meets the right man."

His expression warned Mrs. Reinhardt to pry no further. She linked him as they went in to dinner.

The wind rushed through the chimney and some soot fell on a bouquet of flowers. She saw that. She heard that. She squeezed his arm. They sat opposite. When the wind roars, when the iron catches rattle, when the very windowpanes seem to shiver, when wind and sea combine, then dogs begin to howl and the oncoming storm has a whiff of the supernatural. What does one do, what then does a Mrs. Reinhardt do? One reaches out to the face that is opposite, that one loves, that one hates, that one fears, that one has been betrayed by, that one half knows, that one longs to touch and be reunited with, at least for the duration of a windy night. And by morning who knows? Who knows anything, anyhow.

Adrienne Rich

Poem

SINCE we're not young, weeks have to do time
for years of missing each other. Yet only this odd warp
in time tells me we're not young.
Did I ever walk the morning streets at twenty,
my limbs streaming with a purer joy?
did I lean from any window over the city
listening for the future
as I listen here with nerves tuned for your ring?
And you, you move toward me with the same tempo.
Your eyes are everlasting, the green spark

of the blue-eyed grass of early summer,
the green-blue wild cress washed by the spring.
At twenty, yes: we thought we'd live forever.
At forty-five, I want to know even our limits.
I touch you knowing we weren't born tomorrow,
and somehow, each of us will help the other live,
and somewhere, each of us must help the other die.

May Sarton

Old Lovers at the Ballet

In the dark theatre lovers sit
Watching the supple dancers weave
A fugue, motion and music melded.
There on the stage below, brilliantly lit
No dancer stumbles or may grieve;
Their very smiles are disciplined and moulded.

And in the dark old lovers feel dismay
Watching the ardent bodies leap and freeze,
Thinking how age has changed them and has mocked.

Once they were light and bold in lissome play,
Limber as willows that could bend with ease—
But as they watch a vision is unlocked.

Imagination springs the trap of youth.
And in the dark motionless, as they stare,
Old lovers reach new wonders and new answers
As in the mind they leap to catch the truth,
For young the soul was awkward, unaware,
That claps its hands now with the supple dancers.

And in the flesh those dancers cannot spare
What the old lovers have had time to learn,
That the soul is a lithe and serene athlete
That deepens touch upon the darkening air.
It is not energy but light they burn,
The radiant powers of the Paraclete.

Glenn Busch

John and Muriel Morrison

from You Are My Darling Zita

Muriel

Something else that changed as we got older and which I think was important to us was the way in which we related together physically, the whole sexual thing. In the beginning . . . we were children of our time . . . "inhibited" would be the word. Certainly we were not used to talking about such things, and so for a while it made that part of our lives more difficult. Well, naturally that changed quickly enough, and then in later years it changed again. Now, that was not just a physical thing; it had also to do with us understanding things in terms of the feminist philosophy—the way in which women, and some men, were starting to perceive things then. Looking at this whole question of the male penetration. That it's what the male does with his intellect and with his life, as well as with his penis—and the woman receiving. Well, that's only part of the story. There is a difference. Women, I think, are much—well, let's talk about me—happier to rest in warmth and tenderness. So there was starting to come through then the realisation that the penis and the orgasm were not the be-all and end-all of any sort of togetherness. In fact it often struck me as strange that even if you have orgasm together, it is still a completely self-centred act. What came as a tremendous new realisation at that time was the idea that loving a person didn't always mean sex, not in that manner. In a wider sense there was this greater recognition of the quality of relationships—of relating. The idea that tenderness and concern are also part—and truly part—of sex. I'm not saying of course that women don't enjoy the physicality of sex; no, the thing that was changing then was their awareness about the right to be themselves. Today it is the new woman who is going to say—who is saying—I am not here to serve your purposes. I am here as your partner, your companion, to love, to be loved, but not always just to be available when you want my body. Now, that is an awareness that's growing. That's happening. The ability to work something out that is satisfying for both of you—that is the important thing that's happening. And the amount of concern and consideration you have for one another is what makes it possible.

How you get from one place to the other—how that has happened for me personally—well, I don't think it was any great flash of understanding. No, it was more a blind going forward, discovering through books or films, perhaps, that other people were feeling similar things. And hearing the thing expressed, you were then more able to express it yourself. Partly also it was my own growing . . . the experiences you have . . . all these things come together. Whatever it was it took place over quite a period of time. John and I talked about it a great deal of course, on and off over the years. His being involved in things like marriage guidance and counselling has, I think, made it very much more possible. So that I would talk to him and he would listen to me, sensitively. Lots of other women could talk to their husbands and it would be hopeless. Well, we've been lucky in that.

And now, as we've become older still, the sexual act itself has become very much less. I'm not saying that we shouldn't have it, nor am I speaking for anyone else here, but for myself, as I get older, that need does recede. The sexual act recedes and other things grow stronger. I don't mean there shouldn't be any bodily closeness; certainly there is a need for the physical, for touching, for kissing, hugging, all kinds of gentleness. What we have now is not less intimate, it's just different. I would not say it was a better way than others, that would be wrong. Each person and each couple must find their own way—that is important. This simply is our way, and for us it is good. At our age any sort of pressure to perform is long gone. What feels good for me now is to be relaxed, quiet, and just to enjoy this moment with John. And that is a long way from when we were young. The rush of those times, the pressure, the tension of the possibility of failure—ah, we were funny creatures. Bursting our boilers to get there, and then all the anxiety that ejaculation would come before the right time, trying to control things, orgasm—all those silly stresses that have disappeared along the way. Now there is nothing left of the struggle for oneself, no possessiveness, no urgency. What we have left is a certain peacefulness, the feeling of two bodies together in what I would call a peaceful enjoyment.

THERE IS a thing that happens as you live over a long period of time, at least I feel it has happened to me, and it is simply this—you come to know yourself better. I know better what to do with myself and to myself. And I understand more about seeing myself in others too. The woman who, let's say, talks on incessantly, who would once have annoyed me, I now see that bit of me in her. Now I would stop and think, Ah ha, I am looking at myself. And here is the important thing—take her and love her. She is to be accepted, she is to be embraced, she is not to be cast aside. She is part of you, and without her you are not whole. The dark shadows we see in other people are our own dark shadows. That has been a very important bit of my life and growth—my spiritual life, which means a lot to me. You know, I had a dream once—this would have been when we were at Judge Street, yes. Somewhere in those years between 1969 and 1980, I suppose, and I had this fantastic dream. There was this glorious tree at Judge Street, a copper beech. It was my favourite, a great giant of a tree. Oh, we had to lop off branches, alas; otherwise it would have grown over the whole house. And in my dream there was a man standing beside the tree, and he wanted to speak to me. And so I went to the window, I opened it and looked down—the moon was shining—and I could see on the trunk of the tree an upside-down G. Backwards, it was backwards, a back-to-front G. The man spoke to me then, he said something about going to the moon, and I said I wasn't interested. Then I shut the window, and suddenly I thought, I must go and shut the back door or he'll go around and get in. But as I went towards the door, in the dark passage on the way, I met him face to face. This was a moment of horror . . . and then it was a moment of adjustment, for this was my own dark self. I had to work through this. This was the dark part of me which I was to meet, to recognise, to know, and to embrace.

I woke up then, and I woke John as well to tell him—I had to tell him. I said, "I've had a Jungian dream." An archetypal dream. Well, that dream has been significant to me for the rest of my life. This meeting of my dark self, which has gone on in all sorts of ways. The parts of me I really don't want to look at and see, or admit. The knowledge that there are parts of me I have not wanted to look at . . . well, I could go on, but you know, really it's just the learning process. The things that come to you over time. In fact probably there is no such thing as old age; there are just older people. Yes, just people getting more mature.

JOHN

SOMEBODY once said that life was like jumping off a cliff seventy or eighty years high—the nearer you get to the bottom, the faster it goes. To me I suppose it has been a surprise more than anything—my God, suddenly I am in my seventies—but then really there are no great and sudden differences in that. As a young man I can remember looking forward to the time when I would be twenty-one. It was the adult age, you had the key to the door, and voting rights, and all the rest of it, and I can remember looking forward to that. But when it came it was all an anti-climax, it felt no different. And of course when I knew better—as I got a bit older and reflected on this—it was simply an illusion. And I think the same now. There is no kind of swap-over point, where beforehand you're an adult and then you're an older person. It is not like that, not a discernible change—at least not for me. Perhaps as I say, a surprise, but a surprise that's okay. Life is still enjoyable.

Changes have occurred of course—physical vigour would be one—but often these things have altered so gradually that you hardly notice them. The mountain tramping we once did, not mountain climbing, but pretty arduous stuff, that stopped a few years back. It gradually got less and less as we began to realise we didn't have what it takes anymore. We wouldn't think of it now, not for the last maybe five or six years. We've done day trips, things within our capacity, but yes, that's changed. The structure of my day would be different now as well. Occasionally I'm not so good in the morning, but mostly I'm up at six o'clock and make a cup of tea. I'll meditate first, then off I go and sometimes I work pretty hard. After I've been going a couple of hours, though, it starts to taper off. Well, okay, I'll go and have a rest and a read; then after I've recovered a bit I'll get back to it. And often I'll think to myself, you know, how marvellous it is to be able to do this. I don't mind that I can't work all day as I once could. I'm content with the time that's there, and for the rest of it just to sleep or read, those sorts of things, I'm happy with that. I don't feel I'm missing anything. The only thing at the moment that's not so good is my leg, it's been giving me a bit of bother now and again. And the thought has come to me—you know, say it did hobble me, which it has been doing a little, say it got a bit worse, well, that wouldn't be too good. I wouldn't be able to get into the workshop then, or just generally get about, and that would be hard to take. I suppose I would adjust to it if I had to, just as many other people have, find ways of using the rest of myself. But at the moment—well, I don't know what's going to come of it—it doesn't worry me too much. I'm still fortunate in having good eyesight and hearing, touch, smell, all those things, so my sensual appreciation of the world is still very much alive, which is nice.

There's another thing about the physical at this age as well. I haven't yet perhaps articulated this sufficiently to myself to explain it properly, but—how can I put it? The passions of youth and the constant struggle to adjust, the overwhelming domination of the sexual interest and the coping with all the conflicts that are involved in that . . . that was a difficult aspect of one's living—with my living—and my impression is that it is the same with most people. And so there is something good about the fact that as you get older there is a certain diminution of the sexual aspect of existence. There appears naturally to be a physiological consideration to it, a certain diminishment that can, I believe, lead to a more sophisticated and sensitive companionship. That the purely erotic side of my life is practically gone, that I can now enjoy the subtleties of affection and delight in another person's presence, that I am able to touch or cuddle without the kind of sexual stimulus that was inherent in that at a younger age—that is a tremendous relief. Now, you see, that may be hard for a young person to understand. For a young man to lose his sexual powers, that would be a threat of the highest order. I know from working with younger people that this business of potency for the man was a kind of all-pervasive thing. There was this whole idea that unless they persuaded a woman to sleep with them, or maybe produced a child, then they were inadequate. It's hard for them to understand that you can enjoy relationships at my age in a way that was just never possible before.

There is, I think, a distinction between what you might call caring, and desire. And love in a sense has always been associated with desire. If you just listen to the current songs, the love songs on the radio, there's no question about it. Well, occasionally you might get an element of tenderness or caring for the other person, but by and large it's desire. This kind of sexual chemistry in relationships, a sort of conditioned response that sets people's blood pumping and all sorts of hormonal processes going, just by the sight or sound of something—that sort of thing seems to have gone haywire in our time. Well, maybe it always was. The thing I feel now is that to call desire "love," in any real sense of the word, is nonsense. Maybe a lot of people would disagree with me, but, I mean, if you stand back and take a look at it, just who are you loving in that sort of process? Certainly as far as my own youth was concerned, and with other blokes I knew and talked to, sexual gratification was the operating power behind what we called love. And the crazy thing about that of course—about all these disastrous attempts at the old ideals of sexual achievement and relationships—is that in the end it all seemed so unsatisfactory. And yet on it goes. The whole thing continues to carry on. All through my life, in the work I've been involved with, I have seen this sort of thing upsetting and dominating the lives of so many people. Well, my hope now is that a new time's coming, a time when maybe some of these misconceptions are going to disappear, and it would seem to me it is the women's movement that is showing the way in that direction.

The best that I can assume from women in the feminist movement is that they are absolutely sick of being used as sexual objects. That is something you hear coming through all the time. And the thing that they do value is companionship and affection. The tenderness and kindness and, you know, the respect in the sense of not assuming the use of them. That, I feel, has a high value to them. But as men, by and large, we have been pretty poor on that side of things. You have the classic thing of blokes coming home, tired maybe, and they will go off to bed and have intercourse, and then they will roll over and go to sleep. And the women are left completely and utterly frustrated. Maybe not sexually frustrated, but emotionally frustrated. Perhaps part of the answer to this is tied up in the sort of question that is often asked: "Do you love me?" And from that comes all sorts of superficial answers like "She's so wonderful," "She's just marvellous," "She's so beautiful," and all the rest of it, which can disappear very quickly and often does. Perhaps the question to ask is, "How do I love you?" To look at the way in which we demonstrate that love to another. The consideration, the supportiveness, the touching. You see, the question of "Do you love me?" or "Why do you love me?"—heaven alone knows. But "How do I love you?" "What do I do?"—you can be very clear about that.

There's one other thing I would like to say about this while I'm on it. It often seems with young people that they have a perception of old age—an assumption really—that older people are not sexually active. Now, that's not true. There is perhaps this benchmark of the young, nubile body, which is beautiful in its own way—sure. But I think it needs to be said that while one may lose the bloom of youth, that doesn't mean to say all attractiveness is gone. And one of the delights I've found in growing old is that while our physical appearance is not what it used to be, there is certainly still enjoyment between us. I mean, I might look at Muriel and think, gosh, she's getting a bit ropey around the neck, ha, but, you see, that's beside the point. We don't have to look physically beautiful to get a response of joy and pleasure in one another's company. A cuddle in the nude is still a delightful thing.

Ellen Gilchrist

The Young Man

This is a story about an old lady who ordered a young man from an L. L. Bean catalog. He was a nice young man with wide shoulders and a worried smile. He had on a tweed coat and dark tan pants and a nice-looking tie with little squiggly things all over it. His fingernails were clean and his hair neatly combed. He liked to work but he was also a good companion on trips. His table manners were excellent but not noticeable. He liked to talk but knew how to let the other person have their turn. Mrs. Bradlee never did get around to asking him what his profession was, his line of work. There never did seem to be a polite way to ask.

All of Mrs. Bradlee's friends were getting young men. You could hardly find four for bridge anymore at the Recess Club. Fanny Hawkins had even started dressing like her young man, flat shoes and work pants. Carrie Hatcher pretended her young man was a chauffeur. All they did was drive around talking about themselves. Elsie Whitfield stayed on the coast with hers; they went fishing. It made Mrs. Bradlee sick at her stomach to think of it. One night she dreamed a big Greyhound bus pulled up in front of the old courthouse on State Street and all these young men got out and started spreading out all over Jackson, moving out in all directions. Like a web that had fallen over the world.

Mrs. Bradlee wasn't having anything to do with it. They weren't eating dinner at her house. I've seen enough, she told herself. I've had enough to contend with. Mrs. Bradlee was a widow. She had buried two sons in two wars and a husband from smoking cigarettes. All I want to do from now on is live a normal life, she told her remaining children. So whatever you do, don't tell me about it. Just come over on Sunday after church while you're still covered up.

You shouldn't live alone, her friends were always telling Mrs. Bradlee. She still lived in her house on Lakefront Drive, with all her rooms. They wanted her to get an apartment where they were, at Westchester Arms, or Dunleith Court or Dunsinae Towers. Well, she wasn't going to move into an apartment. She wasn't joining the herd. She had been raised in the country. She had seen one cow lead the rest to water. Still, it was getting lonely in the big stone house. If only it could be like it used to be, with her friends coming over for cards. They had even started bringing the young men to Saint James. Right up to the prayer rail, and beyond. Alece Treadway was sending hers to divinity school.

It was too much. In the past Mrs. Bradlee had been known as the leader. She had been the first to cut her hair at college, the first to have a white cook, the first to get a face-lift (when the time came), the first to visit behind the Iron Curtain. When August, her husband, was still alive. Now, with their craze for young men, the crowd had left her behind.

IT WAS ALL so, well, so messy. And the young men themselves, well, she hated to cast stones, but they were messy too. Well, they were. They wore open-collar sport shirts and tennis sneakers and barely cut their hair. It was too much. It was just too much. Mrs. Bradlee's knitting needles clicked like a thousand crickets. She was alone in her living room. A beautiful sunset was covering the lake with her favorite shades of blue and pink. Elvie Howard had bowed out of their Wednesday night canasta game, now that she had her swimming pool maintenance friend. He has a degree in Philosophy, she told Mrs. Bradlee, from the East. It's television, Mrs. Bradlee decided. That's where they got the ideas. She switched off her own and went into the library to read.

A stack of catalogs was on a table by the windowseat. She began flipping through them, thinking of ordering some clothes for the grandchildren for Christmas. She took a piece of white chocolate from a dish and began to nibble on it, looking at the elegant clothes and shoes and hand-carved decoys, the scarves and ties and stacks of well-made shirts. One model began to catch her eye. He was in several different catalogs. The best picture was on page sixteen of the L. L. Bean catalog. He had such neat hair, his smile was so, well, just right, not too smiley, just enough so you would know he was friendly. His hands were in his pockets. He was standing so tall and straight. I ought to order him, she thought. Laughing to herself out loud. She ate another piece of chocolate. Then another. Hello, she said to the photograph. What's your name?

It was growing dark outside. She pushed a light switch and carried the catalog over to a desk and sat down and took an order blank out of the back and began to fill it in. *One*, she wrote, page 16, number 331, color, white, she paused at where to fill in the amount. $10,000, she wrote and added her Merrill Lynch Visa Card number. There, that should be about right. She folded the order blank in halves, stuck it into its envelope, and carried it across the room to the marble table before the fireplace. She dropped it on a silver salver. Here, Mr. Postman, she said, as if she were a child playing at things, take this letter to the warehouse.

A bell was ringing in the hall. The cook was calling her to dinner.

IN THE MORNING the envelope was gone. "Have you seen an envelope I left in the library?" she said to the maid. "Well, yes, I did," the girl said. "I mailed it for you. In the morning mail."

"Oh, you can't mail that," Mrs. Bradlee said. "It was a joke.

Those people will think I'm crazy when they open that. They'll say, here's a woman in Mississippi who's lost her mind."

"What was it, ma'am?" the maid said.

"I ordered something they don't sell," she said. The two of them laughed together at that. Mrs. Bradlee liked the little maid. An octoroon named Rivers, a sweet girl who was always neat and clean and smelled good.

IT WAS A week later when the young man came. It was nine in the morning. A Sunday morning. Mrs. Bradlee had been up and dressed for an hour, enjoying the fall colors out the windows. She saw him coming up the walk. "You ordered me," he said. "And here I am."

"Go away," she said.

"I can't," he said. "I belong here now. You asked for me. I don't have anyplace else to be."

"Have you had breakfast?" she said.

"No," he said.

"Come in," she said. "I will feed you." It was warm in the breakfast room, filled with morning sunlight. "Do you mind if I take off my coat?" he said. "Oh, no," she answered. "Here, let me take it for you." She took the lovely tweed coat and laid it across an empty chair. It was the cook's day off. She fixed eggs and toast and juice. When he was finished he laid his fork and knife neatly along the edge of the plate. "If you'll excuse me now," he said. "I would like to use your bathroom."

She led the way to the guest room. When he returned she suggested that they go to church. "Mr. Biggs, our choir director, has a special musicale this morning. After morning prayer. You might enjoy that."

"It will be fine," he said. "I'm sure I'll think it's right."

You should have seen the eyes when Mrs. Bradlee walked in with him, walked right up front to her regular pew and he helped her in and pulled down the prayer bench and knelt beside her. Thank you, she heard herself pray, you know I deserved this. The music was grand, clear and cold water running over stones. The whole church and all its people melded together by music, one big melodic pyramid. Afterwards, they stood outside and Mrs. Bradlee introduced him all around.

In the afternoon they took naps in their rooms, then went for a walk around the grounds, down to the lake, and back to the house. He walked at just the right rate of speed, not running ahead of her all the time like August did, saying can't you keep up, if you didn't talk so much you could keep up with me. Larry didn't mind how much Mrs. Bradlee talked. He was interested in everything she said.

"How long are you staying?" she asked finally. It was after dinner. They were having coffee in the den. It seemed like the proper thing to say.

"How long do you want me for?" he asked. He was looking straight at her out of his dark blue eyes. He was looking at her as if there were no wrong answers.

"Let me think about it," she said. "I'm still getting used to the idea."

"Fine," he said. "Whatever you say."

"Where would you go if you left here? Where else would you be?"

"I wouldn't be," he said. "There is only here."

"And you don't mind," she said.

"Why should I mind?" he answered. "That's the way it is."

"I'm going to bed now," she said. "I need to sleep."

"Good night then," he said. "I'll see you in the morning."

IN THE MORNING it was Monday. She dressed before she went downstairs. They had breakfast. "Now you should go to work," she said. "It's Monday morning."

"Fine," he said. "I'll be back at five-thirty."

"Take the blue car," she said. "I don't use it."

"I will," he said. "I like cars to be blue. It's my favorite color." After he was gone Mrs. Bradlee talked on the phone all morning. All her friends called her one by one. What's he like, they asked. He likes blue, she answered. His favorite color is blue. Go fishing with us, Elsie Whitfield said. We might, Mrs. Bradlee answered. I'll have to see. Do you want to? she asked him later. I don't know, he said. Do you? I don't think so, she said. It's so messy. Find a nice way to tell them, he said. Don't hurt their feelings.

Don't you need some other clothes, she said. You might grow tired of that coat. That will be nice, he said. We'll go shopping at the mall.

MANY DAYS went by. Many weeks. Christmas came and went. They gave each other gifts. He gave her a bracelet with her name inside. She gave him a bundle of fatwood sticks she ordered from Maine and a tiny sled containing a gold watch. He put it on. His wrist was so perfect. The hair lay so softly along the flesh. Mrs. Bradlee drew in her breath. For a moment she wanted to kiss his hand. God is love, she thought, and reached out to touch his hand instead. We might go to Switzerland for a month, she said. That would be nice, he said. I think that would be perfect.

IN JANUARY the rain fell and the Pearl River rose and the cold came and stayed. It got into Mrs. Bradlee's bones. She felt tired even in the mornings. Her appetite was not good. When she passed Larry in the hall she sighed. He was there every morning. He was there every afternoon. Every Friday she filled the blue car up with gasoline. Every month the bills came. Every morning after breakfast he disappeared into the guest room. It made her sick at her stomach to think what he did in there.

She began to be cold to him. She was quiet when they went on walks. She stopped telling him everything. After all, what had he ever told her? She was giving him all her stories. In return, all he knew was blue. Blue skies, blue, blue, blue.

"I think you should play the piano," she told him one evening. "It would be a good idea for you to play."

"I'm not a piano player," he said. "That isn't what you asked for."

"You could learn, couldn't you? You could take lessons."

"I'll try," he said. "I'll be glad to try."

"It should sound like this," she said. She took a Mozart sonata out of its cover and put it on the record player. It was sonata number 13 in B major, played by Wanda Landowska. "But that's a woman playing," he said.

"It doesn't matter," Mrs. Bradlee said. "It's all the same thing."

HE WASN'T any good at the piano. He took lessons for three months but nothing happened. His hands were better in his pockets. His hands were better taking the Maine fatwood and using it to light the library fires at night. They were nice laying his knife and fork across his plate after meals. They were too large for the piano or too stiff or too short. Something was wrong. You're disappointed, aren't you, he said at last. Yes, she answered, to tell the truth I am. I think you will have to leave soon. It isn't a good idea anymore. You will have to find somewhere else to go.

How long should I stay, he asked. I don't know the right amount of time.

Until Easter weekend, she said. That should be about right.

Maundy Thursday came. They met for breakfast without speaking of it. He looked pale. Eat, she said. You should eat before your journey.

On Good Friday they went to communion. He looks tired, Fanny Hawkins said to her. He looks like he needs a rest.

On Holy Saturday he walked all around the house, all day, out into the yard, and down along the river. He looked very beautiful, and light. He had not gone into the guest room after breakfast. He had barely eaten anything at all. Mrs. Bradlee was beginning to enjoy him again. He seemed so light, so easy to support.

Perhaps I'll have him stay till summer, she thought, watching his progress across the yard; he was moving toward a line of dogwood trees set against the horizon. Three trees against a blue sky. Yes, I will tell him we will think it over.

The phone rang. It was the refrigerator repairman. What a time to call, she told him. Come Monday. Don't worry about it now. It broke her concentration. She went back to her afghan. She was knitting an afghan to sell at a church bazaar. When Larry came in he walked by without speaking. He did not come down to dinner. I'll talk to him later, she thought. The meal was heavy. She drank too much wine and fell asleep earlier than she expected.

In the morning she went to find him. Of course he was not there. She looked all over the house. She looked in all the closets. She looked in the basement and the wine cellar and the attic. She went out into the garage and looked in the blue car. She went to the guest room. She stood in the door. There was nothing there. The door to the guest-room powder room was open. I could look in there, she thought. But I'm not going to.

She went out into the hall and sat down on the stairs. She listened for the sound of footsteps. She thought about the stars. She said the alphabet over and over to herself. It was a trick she had practiced as a child to pass the time. After a while she went down to the library and got out the new catalogs and began to look through them. I might get a young woman this time, she thought. It was a gay thought. How brave, they would all say. A young woman with all the things that can go wrong. I would like a tall one with a long waist, she decided. Long legs and a long waist. A singing voice. Piano skills.

Gabriel García Márquez

Forever on the *New Fidelity*

from Love in the Time of Cholera

At seven o'clock the first departure warning was sounded, and Fermina Daza felt it resonate with a sharp pain in her left ear. The night before, her dreams had been furrowed with evil omens that she did not dare to decipher. Very early in the morning she had ordered the car to take her to the nearby seminary burial ground, which in those days was called La Manga Cemetery, and as she stood in front of his crypt, she made peace with her dead husband in a monologue in which she freely recounted all the just recriminations she had choked back. Then she told him the details of the trip and said good-bye for now. She refused to tell anyone anything except that she was going away, which is what she had done whenever she had gone to Europe, in order to avoid exhausting farewells. Despite all her travels, she felt as if this were her first trip, and as the day approached her agitation increased. Once she was on board she felt abandoned and sad, and she wanted to be alone to cry.

When the final warning sounded, Dr. Urbino Daza and his wife bade her an undramatic good-bye, and Florentino Ariza accompanied them to the gangplank. Dr. Urbino Daza tried to stand aside so that Florentino Ariza could follow his wife, and only then did he realize that Florentino Ariza was also taking the trip. Dr. Urbino Daza could not hide his confusion.

"But we did not discuss this," he said.

Florentino Ariza showed him the key to his cabin with too evident an intention: an ordinary cabin on the common deck. But to Dr. Urbino Daza this did not seem sufficient proof of innocence. He glanced at his wife in consternation, with the eyes of a drowning man looking for support, but her eyes were ice. She said in a very low, harsh voice: "You too?" Yes: he too, like his sister Ofelia, thought there was an age at which love began to be indecent. But he was able to recover in time, and he said good-bye to Florentino Ariza with a handshake that was more resigned than grateful.

From the railing of the salon, Florentino Ariza watched them disembark. Just as he had hoped and wished, Dr. Urbino Daza and his wife turned to look at him before climbing into their automobile, and he waved his hand in farewell. They both responded in kind. He remained at the railing until the automobile disappeared in the dust of the freight yard, and then he went to his cabin to change into clothing more suitable for his first dinner on board in the Captain's private dining room.

It was a splendid evening, which Captain Diego Samaritano seasoned with succulent tales of his forty years on the river, but Fermina Daza had to make an enormous effort to appear amused. Despite the fact that the final warning had been sounded at eight o'clock, when visitors had been obliged to leave and the gangplank had been raised, the boat did not set sail until the Captain had finished eating and gone up to the bridge to direct the operation. Fermina Daza and Florentino Ariza stayed at the railing, surrounded by noisy passengers who made bets on how well they could identify the lights in the city, until the boat sailed out of the bay, moved along invisible channels and through swamps spattered with the undulating lights of the fishermen, and at last took a deep breath in the open air of the Great Magdalena River. Then the band burst into a popular tune, there was a joyous stampede of passengers, and in a mad rush, the dancing began.

Fermina Daza preferred to take refuge in her cabin. She had not said a word for the entire evening, and Florentino Ariza allowed her to remain lost in her thoughts. He interrupted her only to say good night outside her cabin, but she was not tired, just a little chilly, and she suggested that they sit for a while on her private deck to watch the river. Florentino Ariza wheeled two wicker easy chairs to the railing, turned off the lights, placed a woolen shawl around her shoulders, and sat down beside her. With surprising skill, she rolled a cigarette from the little box of tobacco that he had brought her. She smoked it slowly, with the lit end inside her mouth, not speaking, and then she rolled another two and smoked them one right after the other. Sip by sip, Florentino Ariza drank two thermoses of mountain coffee.

The lights of the city had disappeared over the horizon. Seen from the darkened deck in the light of a full moon, the smooth, silent river and the pastureland on either bank became a phosphorescent plain. From time to time one could see a straw hut next to the great bonfires signaling that wood for the ships' boilers was on sale. Florentino Ariza still had dim memories of the journey of his youth, and in dazzling flashes of lightning the sight of the river called them back to life as if they had happened yesterday. He recounted some of them to Fermina Daza in the belief that this might animate her, but she sat smoking in another world. Florentino Ariza renounced his memories and left her alone with hers, and in the meantime he rolled cigarettes and passed them to her already lit, until the box was empty. The music stopped after midnight, the voices of the passengers dispersed and broke into sleepy whispers, and two hearts, alone in the shadows on the deck, were beating in time to the breathing of the ship.

After a long while, Florentino Ariza looked at Fermina Daza by the light of the river. She seemed ghostly, her sculptured profile softened by a tenuous blue light, and he realized that she was crying in silence. But instead of consoling her or waiting until all her tears had been shed, which is what she wanted, he allowed panic to overcome him.

"Do you want to be alone?" he asked.

"If I did, I would not have told you to come in," she said.

Then he reached out with two icy fingers in the darkness, felt for the other hand in the darkness, and found it waiting for him. Both were lucid enough to realize, at the same fleeting instant, that the hands made of old bones were not the hands they had imagined before touching. In the next moment, however, they were. She began to speak of her dead husband in the present tense, as if he were alive, and Florentino Ariza knew then that for her, too, the time had come to ask herself with dignity, with majesty, with an irrepressible desire to live, what she should do with the love that had been left behind without a master.

Fermina Daza stopped smoking in order not to let go of the hand that was still in hers. She was lost in her longing to understand. She could not conceive of a husband better than hers had been, and yet when she recalled their life she found more difficulties than pleasures, too many mutual misunderstandings, useless arguments, unresolved angers. Suddenly she sighed: "It is incredible how one can be happy for so many years in the midst of so many squabbles, so many problems, damn it, and not really know if it was love or not." By the time she finished unburdening herself, someone had turned off the moon. The boat moved ahead at its steady pace, one foot in front of the other: an immense, watchful animal. Fermina Daza had returned from her longing.

"Go now," she said.

Florentino Ariza pressed her hand, bent toward her, and tried to kiss her on the cheek. But she refused, in her hoarse, soft voice.

"Not now," she said to him. "I smell like an old woman."

She heard him leave in the darkness, she heard his steps on the stairs, she heard him cease to exist until the next day. Fermina Daza lit another cigarette, and as she smoked she saw Dr. Juvenal Urbino in his immaculate linen suit, with his professional rigor, his dazzling charm, his official love, and he tipped his white hat in a gesture of farewell from another boat out of the past. "We men are the miserable slaves of prejudice," he had once said to her. "But when a woman decides to sleep with a man, there is no wall she will not scale, no fortress she will not destroy, no moral consideration she will not ignore at its very root: there is no God worth worrying about." Fermina Daza sat motionless until dawn, thinking about Florentino Ariza, not as the desolate sentinel in the little Park of the Evangels, whose memory did not awaken even a spark of nostalgia in her, but as he was now, old and lame, but real: the man who had always been within reach and whom she could never acknowledge. As the breathing boat carried her toward the splendor of the day's first roses, all that she asked of God was that Florentino Ariza would know how to begin again the next day.

He did. Fermina Daza instructed the steward to let her sleep as long as she wanted, and when she awoke there was a vase on the night table with a fresh white rose, drops of dew still on it, as well as a letter from Florentino Ariza with as many pages as he had written since his farewell to her. It was a calm letter that did not attempt to do more than express the state of mind that had held him captive since the previous night: it was as lyrical as the others, as rhetorical as all of them, but it had a foundation in reality. Fermina Daza read it with some embarrassment because of the shameless racing of her heart. It concluded with the request that she advise the steward when she was ready, for the Captain was waiting on the bridge to show them the operation of the ship.

She was ready at eleven o'clock, bathed and smelling of flower-scented soap, wearing a very simple widow's dress of gray etamine, and completely recovered from the night's turmoil. She ordered a sober breakfast from the steward, who was dressed in impeccable white, and in the Captain's personal service, but she did not send a message for anyone to come for her. She went up alone, dazzled by the cloudless sky, and she found Florentino Ariza talking to the Captain on the bridge. He looked different to her, not only because she saw him now with other eyes, but because in reality he had changed. Instead of the funereal clothing he had worn all his life, he was dressed in comfortable white shoes, slacks, and a linen shirt with an open collar, short sleeves, and his monogram embroidered on the breast pocket. He also had on a white Scottish cap and removable dark lenses over his perpetual eyeglasses for myopia. It was evident that everything was being used for the first time and had been bought just for the trip, with the exception of the well-worn belt of dark brown leather, which Fermina Daza noticed at first glance as if it were a fly in the soup. Seeing him like this, dressed just for her in so patent a manner, she could not hold back the fiery blush that rose to her face. She was embarrassed when she greeted him, and he was more embarrassed by her embarrassment. The knowledge that they were behaving as if they were sweethearts was even more embarrassing, and the knowledge that they were both embarrassed embarrassed them so much that Captain Samaritano noticed it with a tremor of compassion. He extricated them from their difficulty by spending the next two hours explaining the controls and the general operation of the ship. They were sailing very slowly up a river without banks that meandered between arid sandbars stretching to the horizon. But unlike the troubled waters at the mouth of the river, these were slow and clear and gleamed like metal under the merciless sun. Fermina Daza had the impression that it was a delta filled with islands of sand.

"It is all the river we have left," said the Captain.

Florentino Ariza, in fact, was surprised by the changes, and would be even more surprised the following day, when navigation became more difficult and he realized that the Magdalena, father of waters, one of the great rivers of the world, was only an illusion of memory. Captain Samaritano explained to them how fifty years of uncontrolled deforestation had destroyed the river: the boilers of the riverboats had consumed the thick forest of colossal trees that had oppressed Florentino Ariza on his first voyage. Fermina Daza would not see the animals of her dreams: the hunters for skins from the tanneries in New Orleans had exterminated the alligators that, with yawning mouths, had played dead for hours on end in the gullies along the shore as they lay in wait for butterflies; the parrots with their shrieking and the monkeys with their lunatic screams had died out as the foliage was destroyed; the manatees with their great breasts that had nursed their young and wept on the banks in a forlorn woman's voice were an extinct species, annihilated by the armored bullets of hunters for sport.

Captain Samaritano had an almost maternal affection for the manatees, because they seemed to him like ladies damned by some extravagant love, and he believed the truth of the legend that they were the only females in the animal kingdom that had no mates. He had always opposed shooting at them from the ship, which was the custom despite the laws prohibiting it. Once, a hunter from North Carolina, his papers in order, had disobeyed him, and with a well-aimed bullet from his Springfield rifle had shattered the head of a manatee mother whose baby became frantic with grief as it wailed over the fallen body. The Captain had the orphan brought on board so that he could care for it, and left the hunter behind on the deserted bank, next to the corpse of the murdered mother. He spent six months in prison as the result of diplomatic protests and almost lost his navigator's license, but he came out prepared to do it again, as often as the need arose. Still, that had been a historic episode: the orphaned manatee, which grew up and lived for many years in the rare-animal zoo in San Nicolás de las Barrancas, was the last of its kind seen along the river.

"Each time I pass that bank," he said, "I pray to God that the gringo will board my ship so that I can leave him behind all over again."

Fermina Daza, who had felt no fondness for the Captain, was so moved by the tenderhearted giant that from that morning on he occupied a privileged place in her heart. She was not wrong: the trip was just beginning, and she would have many occasions to realize that she had not been mistaken.

Fermina Daza and Florentino Ariza remained on the bridge until it was time for lunch. It was served a short while after they passed the town of Calamar on the opposite shore, which just a few years before had celebrated a perpetual fiesta and now was a ruined port with deserted streets. The only creature they saw from the boat was a woman dressed in white, signaling to them with a handkerchief. Fermina Daza could not understand why she was not picked up when she seemed so distressed, but the Captain explained that she was the ghost of a drowned woman whose deceptive signals were intended to lure ships off course into the dangerous whirlpools along the other bank. They passed so close that Fermina Daza saw her in sharp detail in the sunlight, and she had no doubt that she did not exist, but her face seemed familiar.

It was a long, hot day. Fermina Daza returned to her cabin after lunch for her inevitable siesta, but she did not sleep well because of a pain in her ear, which became worse when the boat exchanged mandatory greetings with another R.C.C. vessel as they passed each other a few leagues above Barranca Vieja. Florentino Ariza fell into instantaneous sleep in the main salon, where most of the passengers without cabins were sleeping as if it were midnight, and close to the spot where he had seen her disembark, he dreamed of Rosalba. She was traveling alone, wearing her Mompox costume from the last century, and it was she and not the child who slept in the wicker cage that hung from the ceiling. It was a dream at once so enigmatic and so amusing that he enjoyed it for the rest of the afternoon as he played dominoes with the Captain and two of the passengers who were friends of his.

It grew cooler as the sun went down, and the ship came back to life. The passengers seemed to emerge from a trance; they had just bathed and changed into fresh clothing, and they sat in the wicker armchairs in the salon, waiting for supper, which was announced at exactly five o'clock by a waiter who walked the deck from one end to the other and rang a sacristan's bell, to mocking applause. While they were eating, the band began to play fandangos, and the dancing continued until midnight.

Fermina Daza did not care to eat because of the pain in her ear, and she watched as the first load of wood for the boilers was taken on from a bare gully where there was nothing but stacked logs and a very old man who supervised the operation. There did not seem to be another person for many leagues around. For Fermina Daza it was a long, tedious stop that would have been unthinkable on the ocean liners to Europe, and the heat was so intense that she could feel it even on her cooled observation deck. But when the boat weighed anchor again there was a cool breeze scented with the heart of the forest, and the music became more lively. In the town of Sitio Nuevo there was only one light in only one window in only one house, and the port office did not signal either cargo or passengers, so the boat passed by without a greeting.

Fermina Daza had spent the entire afternoon wondering what

stratagems Florentino Ariza would use to see her without knocking at her cabin door, and by eight o'clock she could no longer bear the longing to be with him. She went out into the passageway, hoping to meet him in what would seem a casual encounter, and she did not have to go very far: Florentino Ariza was sitting on a bench in the passageway, as silent and forlorn as he had been in the Park of the Evangels, and for over two hours he had been asking himself how he was going to see her. They both made the same gesture of surprise that they both knew was feigned, and together they strolled the first-class deck, crowded with young people, most of them boisterous students who, with some eagerness, were exhausting themselves in the final fling of their vacation. In the lounge, Florentino Ariza and Fermina Daza sat at the bar as if they were students themselves and drank bottled soft drinks, and suddenly she saw herself in a frightening situation. She said: "How awful!" Florentino Ariza asked her what she was thinking that caused her so much distress.

"The poor old couple," she said. "The ones who were beaten to death in the boat."

They both decided to turn in when the music stopped, after a long, untroubled conversation on the dark observation deck. There was no moon, the sky was cloudy, and on the horizon flashes of lightning, with no claps of thunder, illuminated them for an instant. Florentino Ariza rolled cigarettes for her, but she did not smoke more than a few, for she was tormented by pain that would ease for a few moments and flare up again when the boat bellowed as it passed another ship or a sleeping village, or when it slowed to sound the depth of the river. He told her with what longing he had watched her at the Poetic Festival, on the balloon flight, on the acrobat's velocipede, with what longing he had waited all year for public festivals just so he could see her. She had often seen him as well, and she had never imagined that he was there only to see her. However, it was less than a year since she had read his letters and wondered how it was possible that he had never competed in the Poetic Festival: there was no doubt he would have won. Florentino Ariza lied to her: he wrote only for her, verses for her, and only he read them. Then it was she who reached for his hand in the darkness, and she did not find it waiting for her as she had waited for his the night before. Instead, she took him by surprise, and Florentino Ariza's heart froze.

"How strange women are," he said.

She burst into laughter, a deep laugh like a young dove's, and she thought again about the old couple in the boat. It was incised: the image would always pursue her. But that night she could bear it because she felt untroubled and calm, as she had few times in her life: free of all blame. She would have remained there until dawn, silent, with his hand perspiring ice into hers, but she could not endure the torment in her ear. So that when the music was over, and then the bustle of the ordinary passengers hanging their hammocks in the salon had ended, she realized that her pain was stronger than her desire to be with him. She knew that telling him about it would alleviate her suffering, but she did not because she did not want to worry him. For now it seemed to her that she knew him as well as if she had lived with him all her life, and she thought him capable of ordering the boat back to port if that would relieve her pain.

Florentino Ariza had foreseen how things would be that night, and he withdrew. At the door of her cabin he tried to kiss her good night, but she offered him her left cheek. He insisted, with labored breath, and she offered him her other cheek, with a coquettishness that he had not known when she was a schoolgirl. Then he insisted again, and she offered him her lips, she offered her lips with a profound trembling that she tried to suppress with the laugh she had forgotten after her wedding night.

"My God," she said, "ships make me so crazy."

Florentino Ariza shuddered: as she herself had said, she had the sour smell of old age. Still, as he walked to his cabin, making his way through the labyrinth of sleeping hammocks, he consoled himself with the thought that he must give off the same odor, except his was four years older, and she must have detected it on him, with the same emotion. It was the smell of human fermentation, which he had perceived in his oldest lovers and they had detected in him. The Widow Nazaret, who kept nothing to herself, had told him in a cruder way: "Now we stink like a henhouse." They tolerated each other because they were an even match: my odor against yours. On the other hand, he had often taken care of América Vicuña, whose diaper smell awakened maternal instincts in him, but he was disturbed at the idea that she had disliked his odor: the smell of a dirty old man. But all that belonged to the past. The important thing was that not since the afternoon when Aunt Escolástica left her missal on the counter in the telegraph office had Florentino Ariza felt the happiness he felt that night: so intense it frightened him.

At five o'clock he was beginning to doze off, when the ship's purser woke him in the port of Zambrano to hand him an urgent telegram. It was signed by Leona Cassiani and dated the previous day, and all its horror was contained in a single line: *América Vicuña dead yesterday reasons unknown.* At eleven o'clock in the morning he learned the details from Leona Cassiani in a telegraphic conference during which he himself operated the transmitting equipment for the first time since his years as a telegraph operator. América Vicuña, in the grip of mortal depression because she had failed her final examinations, had drunk a flask of laudanum stolen from the school infirmary. Florentino Ariza knew in the depths of his soul that the story was incomplete. But no: América Vicuña had left no explanatory note that would have allowed anyone to be blamed for her decision. The family, informed by Leona Cassiani, was arriving now from Puerto Padre, and the funeral would take place that afternoon at five o'clock. Florentino Ariza took a breath. The only thing he could do to stay alive was not to allow himself the anguish of that memory. He erased it from his mind, although from time to time in the years that were left to him he would feel it revive, with no warning and for no reason, like the sudden pang of an old scar.

The days that followed were hot and interminable. The river became muddy and narrow, and instead of the tangle of colossal trees that had astonished Florentino Ariza on his first voyage, there were calcinated flatlands stripped of entire forests that had been devoured by the boilers of the riverboats, and the debris of godforsaken villages whose streets remained flooded even in the cruelest droughts. At night they were awakened not by the siren songs of manatees on the sandy banks but by the nauseating stench of corpses floating down to the sea. For there were no more wars or epidemics, but the swollen bodies still floated by. The Captain, for once, was solemn: "We have orders to tell the passengers that they are accidental drowning victims." Instead of the screeching of the parrots and the riotous noise of invisible monkeys, which at one time had intensified the stifling midday heat, all that was left was the vast silence of the ravaged land.

There were so few places for taking on wood, and they were so far apart from each other, that by the fourth day of the trip the *New Fidelity* had run out of fuel. She was stranded for almost a week while her crew searched bogs of ashes for the last scattered trees. There was no one else: the woodcutters had abandoned their trails, fleeing the ferocity of the lords of the earth, fleeing the invisible cholera, fleeing the larval wars that governments were bent on hiding with distracted decrees. In the meantime, the passengers in their boredom held swimming contests, organized hunting expeditions, and returned with live iguanas that they split open from top to bottom and sewed up again with baling needles after removing the clusters of soft, translucent eggs that they strung over the railings to dry. The poverty-stricken prostitutes from nearby villages followed in the path of the expeditions, improvised tents in the gullies along the shore, brought music and liquor with them, and caroused across the river from the stranded vessel.

Long before he became President of the R.C.C., Florentino Ariza had received alarming reports on the state of the river, but he barely read them. He would calm his associates: "Don't worry, by the time the wood is gone there will be boats fueled by oil." With his mind clouded by his passion for Fermina Daza, he never took the trouble to think about it, and by the time he realized the truth, there was nothing anyone could do except bring in a new river. Even in the days when the waters were at their best, the boats had to anchor at night, and then even the simple fact of being alive became unendurable. Most of the passengers, above all the Europeans, abandoned the pestilential stench of their cabins and spent the night walking the decks, brushing away all sorts of predatory creatures with the same towel they used to dry their incessant perspiration, and at dawn they were exhausted and swollen with bites. An English traveler at the beginning of the nineteenth century, referring to the journey by canoe and mule that could last as long as fifty days, had written: "This is one of the most miserable and uncomfortable pilgrimages that a human being can make." This had no longer been true during the first eighty years of steam navigation, and then it became true again forever when the alligators ate the last butterfly and the maternal manatees were gone, the parrots, the monkeys, the villages were gone: everything was gone.

"There's no problem," the Captain laughed. "In a few years, we'll ride the dry riverbed in luxury automobiles."

For the first three days Fermina Daza and Florentino Ariza were protected by the soft springtime of the enclosed observation deck, but when the wood was rationed and the cooling system began to fail, the Presidential Suite became a steam bath. She survived the nights because of the river breeze that came in through the open windows, and she frightened off the mosquitoes with a towel because the insecticide bomb was useless when the boat was anchored. Her earache had become unbearable, and one morning when she awoke it stopped suddenly and completely, like the sound of a smashed cicada. But she did not realize that she had lost the hearing in her left ear until that night, when Florentino Ariza spoke to her on that side and she had to turn her head to hear what he was saying. She did not tell anyone, for she was resigned to the fact that it was one of the many irremediable defects of old age.

In spite of everything, the delay had been a providential accident for them. Florentino Ariza had once read: "Love becomes greater and nobler in calamity." The humidity in the Presidential Suite submerged them in an unreal lethargy in which it was easier to love without questions. They spent unimaginable hours holding hands in the armchairs by the railing, they exchanged unhurried kisses, they enjoyed the rapture of caresses without the pitfalls of impatience. On the third stupefying night she waited for him with a bottle of anisette, which she used to drink in secret with Cousin Hildebranda's band and later, after she was married and had children, behind closed doors with the friends from her borrowed world. She needed to be somewhat intoxicated in order not to think about her fate with too much lucidity, but Florentino Ariza thought it was to give herself courage for the final step. Encouraged by that illusion, he dared to explore her withered neck with his fingertips, her bosom armored in metal stays, her hips with their decaying bones, her thighs with their aging veins. She accepted with pleasure, her eyes closed, but she did not tremble, and she smoked and drank at regular intervals. At last, when his caresses slid over her belly, she had enough anisette in her heart.

"If we're going to do it, let's do it," she said, "but let's do it like grownups."

She took him to the bedroom and, with the lights on, began to undress without false modesty. Florentino Ariza was on the bed, lying on his back and trying to regain control, once again not knowing what to do with the skin of the tiger he had slain. She said: "Don't look." He asked why without taking his eyes off the ceiling.

"Because you won't like it," she said.

Then he looked at her and saw her naked to her waist, just as he had imagined her. Her shoulders were wrinkled, her breasts sagged, her ribs were covered by a flabby skin as pale and cold as a frog's. She covered her chest with the blouse she had just taken off, and she turned out the light. Then he sat up and began to undress in the darkness, throwing everything at her that he took off, while she tossed it back, dying of laughter.

They lay on their backs for a long time, he more and more perturbed as his intoxication left him, and she peaceful, almost without will, but praying to God that she would not laugh like a fool, as she always did when she overindulged in anisette. They talked to pass the time. They spoke of themselves, of their divergent lives, of the incredible coincidence of their lying naked in a dark cabin on a stranded boat when reason told them they had time only for death. She had never heard of his having a woman, not even one, in that city where everything was known even before it happened. She spoke in a casual manner, and he replied without hesitation in a steady voice:

"I've remained a virgin for you."

She would not have believed it in any event, even if it had been true, because his love letters were composed of similar phrases whose meaning mattered less than their brilliance. But she liked the spirited way in which he said it. Florentino Ariza, for his part, suddenly asked himself what he would never have dared to ask himself before: what kind of secret life had she led outside of her marriage? Nothing would have surprised him, because he knew that women are just like men in their secret adventures: the same stratagems, the same sudden inspirations, the same betrayals without remorse. But he was wise not to ask the question. Once, when her relations with the Church were already strained, her confessor had asked her out of the blue if she had ever been unfaithful to her husband, and she had stood up without responding, without concluding, without saying good-bye, and had never gone to confession again, with that confessor or with any other. But Florentino Ariza's prudence had an unexpected reward: she stretched out her hand in the darkness, caressed his belly, his flanks, his almost hairless pubis. She said: "You have skin like a baby's." Then she took the final step: she searched for him where he was not, she searched again without hope, and she found him, unarmed.

"It's dead," he said.

It had happened to him sometimes, and he had learned to live with the phantom: each time he had to learn again, as if it were the first time. He took her hand and laid it on his chest: Fermina Daza felt the old, untiring heart almost bursting through his skin, beating with the strength, the rapidity, the irregularity of an adolescent's. He said: "Too much love is as bad for this as no love at all." But he said it without conviction: he was ashamed, furious with himself, longing for some reason to blame her for his failure. She knew it, and began to provoke his defenseless body with mock caresses, like a kitten delighting in cruelty, until he could no longer endure the martyrdom and he returned to his cabin. She thought about him until dawn, convinced at last of her love, and as the anisette left her in slow waves, she was invaded by the anguished fear that he was angry and would never return.

But he returned the same day, refreshed and renewed, at the unusual hour of eleven o'clock, and he undressed in front of her with a certain ostentation. She was pleased to see him in the light just as she had imagined him in the darkness: an ageless man, with dark skin that was as shiny and tight as an opened umbrella, with no hair except for a few limp strands under his arms and at his groin. His guard was up, and she realized that he did not expose his weapon by accident, but displayed it as if it were a war trophy in order to give himself courage. He did not even give her time to take off the nightgown that she had put on when the dawn breeze began to blow, and his beginner's haste made her shiver with compassion. But that did not disturb her, because in such cases it was not easy to distinguish between compassion and love. When it was over, however, she felt empty.

It was the first time she had made love in over twenty years, and she had been held back by her curiosity concerning how it would feel at her age after so long a respite. But he had not given her time to find out if her body loved him too. It had been hurried and sad, and she thought: Now we've screwed up everything. But she was wrong: despite the disappointment that each of them felt, despite his regret for his clumsiness and her remorse for the madness of the anisette, they were not apart for a moment in the days that followed. Captain Samaritano, who uncovered by instinct any secret that anyone wanted to keep on his ship, sent them a white rose every morning, had them serenaded with old waltzes from their day, had meals prepared for them with aphrodisiac ingredients as a joke. They did not try to make love again until much later, when the inspiration came to them without their looking for it. They were satisfied with the simple joy of being together.

They would not have thought of leaving the cabin if the Captain had not written them a note informing them that after lunch they would reach golden La Dorada, the last port on the eleven-day journey. From the cabin Fermina Daza and Florentino Ariza saw the promontory of houses lit by a pale sun, and they thought they understood the reason for its name, but it seemed less evident to them when they felt the heat that steamed like a caldron and saw the tar bubbling in the streets. Moreover, the boat did not dock there but on the opposite bank, where the terminal for the Santa Fé railroad was located.

They left their refuge as soon as the passengers disembarked. Fermina Daza breathed the good air of impunity in the empty salon, and from the gunwale they both watched a noisy crowd of people gathering their luggage in the cars of a train that looked like a toy. One would have thought they had come from Europe, above all the women, in their Nordic coats and hats from the last century that made no sense in the sweltering, dusty heat. Some wore beautiful potato blossoms in their hair, but they had begun to wither in the heat. They had just come from the Andean plateau after a train trip through a dreamlike savannah, and they had not had time to change their clothes for the Caribbean.

In the middle of the bustling market, a very old man with an inconsolable expression on his face was pulling chicks out of the pockets of his beggar's coat. He had appeared without warning, making his way through the crowd in a tattered overcoat that had belonged to someone much taller and heavier than he. He took off his hat, placed it brim up on the dock in case anyone wanted to throw him a coin, and began to empty his pockets of handfuls of pale baby chicks that seemed to proliferate in his fingers. In only a moment the dock appeared to be carpeted with cheeping chicks running everywhere among hurried travelers who trampled them without realizing it. Fascinated by the marvelous spectacle that seemed to be performed in her honor, for she was the only person watching it, Fermina Daza did not notice when the passengers for the return trip began to come on board. The party was over: among them she saw many faces she knew, some of them friends who until a short while ago had attended her in her grief, and she rushed to take refuge in her cabin. Florentino Ariza found her there, distraught: she would rather die than be seen on a pleasure trip, by people she knew, so soon after the death of her husband. Her preoccupation affected Florentino Ariza so much that he promised to think of some way to protect her other than keeping her in the cabin.

The idea came to him all at once as they were having supper in the private dining room. The Captain was troubled by a problem he had wanted to discuss for a long time with Florentino Ariza, who always evaded him with his usual answer: "Leona Cassiani can handle those problems better than I can." This time, however, he listened to him. The fact was that the boats carried cargo upriver, but came back empty, while the opposite occurred with passengers. "And the advantage of cargo is that it pays more and eats nothing," he said. Fermina Daza, bored with the men's enervated discussion concerning the possibility of establishing differential fares, ate without will. But Florentino Ariza pursued the discussion to its end, and only then did he ask the question that the Captain thought was the prelude to a solution:

"And speaking hypothetically," he said, "would it be possible to make a trip without stopping, without cargo or passengers, without coming into any port, without anything?"

The Captain said that it was possible, but only hypothetically. The R.C.C. had business commitments that Florentino Ariza was more familiar with than he was, it had contracts for cargo, passengers, mail, and a great deal more, and most of them were unbreakable. The only thing that would allow them to bypass all that was a case of cholera on board. The ship would be quarantined, it would hoist the yellow flag and sail in a state of emergency. Captain Samaritano had needed to do just that on several occasions because of the many cases of cholera along the river, although later the health authorities had obliged the doctors to sign death certificates that called the cases common dysentery. Besides, many times in the history of the river the yellow plague flag had been flown in order to evade taxes, or to avoid picking up an undesirable passenger, or to elude inopportune inspections. Florentino Ariza reached for Fermina Daza's hand under the table.

"Well, then," he said, "let's do that."

The Captain was taken by surprise, but then, with the instinct of an old fox, he saw everything clearly.

"I command on this ship, but you command us," he said. "So if you are serious, give me the order in writing and we will leave right now."

Florentino Ariza was serious, of course, and he signed the order. After all, everyone knew that the time of cholera had not ended despite all the joyful statistics from the health officials. As for the ship, there was no problem. The little cargo they had taken on was transferred, they told the passengers there had been a mechanical failure, and early that morning they sent them on their way on a ship that belonged to another company. If such things were done for so many immoral, even contemptible reasons, Florentino Ariza could not see why it would not be legitimate to do them for love. All that the Captain asked was that they stop in Puerto Nare to pick up someone who would accompany him on the voyage: he, too, had his secret heart.

So the *New Fidelity* weighed anchor at dawn the next day, without cargo or passengers, and with the yellow cholera flag waving jubilantly from the mainmast. At dusk in Puerto Nare they picked up a woman who was even taller and stouter than the Captain, an uncommon beauty who needed only a beard to be hired by a circus. Her name was Zenaida Neves, but the Captain called her "my wild woman": an old friend whom he would pick up in one port and leave in another, and who came on board followed by the winds of joy. In that sad place of death, where Florentino Ariza relived his memories of Rosalba when he saw the train from Envigado struggling to climb the old mule trail, there was an Amazonian downpour that would continue with very few pauses for the rest of the trip. But no one cared: the floating fiesta had its own roof. That night, as a personal contribution to the revelry, Fermina Daza went down to the galley amid the ovations of the crew and prepared a dish for everyone that she created and that Florentino Ariza christened Eggplant al Amor.

During the day they played cards, ate until they were bursting, took gritty siestas that left them exhausted, and as soon as the sun was down the orchestra began to play, and they had anisette with salmon until they could eat and drink no more. It was a rapid journey: the boat was light and the currents favorable and even improved by the floods that rushed down from the headwaters, where it rained as much that week as it had during the entire voyage. Some villages fired charitable cannons for them to frighten away the cholera, and they expressed their gratitude with a mournful bellow. The ships they passed on the way, regardless of the company they belonged to, signaled their condolences. In the town of Magangué, where Mercedes was born, they took on enough wood for the rest of the trip.

Fermina Daza was horrified when she heard the boat's horn with her good ear, but by the second day of anisette she could hear better with both of them. She discovered that roses were more fragrant than before, that the birds sang at dawn much better than before, and that God had created a manatee and placed it on the bank at Tamalameque just so it could awaken her. The Captain heard it, had the boat change course, and at last they saw the enormous matron nursing the baby that she held in her arms. Neither Florentino nor Fermina was aware of how well they understood each other: she helped him to take his enemas, she got up before he did to brush the false teeth he kept in a glass while he slept, and she solved the problem of her misplaced spectacles, for she could use his for reading and mending. When she awoke one morning, she saw him sewing a button on his shirt in the darkness, and she hurried to do it for him before he could say the ritual phrase about needing two wives. On the other hand, the only thing she needed from him was that he cup a pain in her back.

Florentino Ariza, for his part, began to revive old memories with a violin borrowed from the orchestra, and in half a day he could play the waltz of "The Crowned Goddess" for her, and he played it for hours until they forced him to stop. One night, for the first time in her life, Fermina Daza suddenly awoke choking on tears of sorrow, not of rage, at the memory of the old couple in the boat beaten to death by the boatman. On the other hand, the incessant rain did not affect her, and she thought too late that perhaps Paris was not as gloomy as it had seemed, that Santa Fé did not have so many funerals passing along the streets. The dream of other voyages with Florentino Ariza appeared on the horizon: mad voyages, free of trunks, free of social commitments: voyages of love.

The night before their arrival they had a grand party with paper garlands and colored lights. The weather cleared at nightfall. Holding each other very close, the Captain and Zenaida danced the first boleros that were just beginning to break hearts in those days. Florentino Ariza dared to suggest to Fermina Daza that they dance their private waltz, but she refused. Nevertheless she kept time with her head and her heels all night, and there was even a moment when she danced sitting down without realizing it, while the Captain merged with his young wild woman in the shadows of the bolero. She drank so much anisette that she had to be helped up the stairs, and she suffered an attack of laughing until she cried, which alarmed everyone. However, when at last she recovered her self-possession in the perfumed oasis of her cabin, they made the tranquil, wholesome love of experienced grandparents, which she would keep as her best memory of that lunatic voyage. Contrary to what the Captain and Zenaida supposed, they no longer felt like newlyweds, and even less like belated lovers. It was as if they had leapt over the arduous calvary of conjugal life and gone straight to the heart of love. They were together in silence like an old married couple wary of life, beyond the pitfalls of passion, beyond the brutal mockery of hope and the phantoms of disillusion: beyond love. For they had lived together long enough to know that love was always love, anytime and anyplace, but it was more solid the closer it came to death.

They awoke at six o'clock. She had a headache scented with anisette, and her heart was stunned by the impression that Dr. Juvenal Urbino had come back, plumper and younger than when he had fallen from the tree, and that he was sitting in his rocking chair, waiting for her at the door of their house. She was, however, lucid enough to realize that this was the result not of the anisette but of her imminent return.

"It is going to be like dying," she said.

Florentino Ariza was startled, because her words read a thought that had given him no peace since the beginning of the voyage home. Neither one could imagine being in any other home but the cabin, or eating in any other way but on the ship, or living any other life, for that would be alien to them forever. It was, indeed, like dying. He could not go back to sleep. He lay on his back in bed, his hands crossed behind his head. At a certain moment, the pangs of grief for América Vicuña made him twist with pain, and he could not hold off the truth any longer: he locked himself in the bathroom and cried, slowly, until his last tear was shed. Only then did he have the courage to admit to himself how much he had loved her.

When they went up, already dressed for going ashore, the ship had left behind the narrow channels and marshes of the old Spanish passage and was navigating around the wrecks of boats and the platforms of oil wells in the bay. A radiant Thursday was breaking over the golden domes of the city of the Viceroys, but Fermina Daza, standing at the railing, could not bear the pestilential stink of its glories, the arrogance of its bulwarks profaned by iguanas: the horror of real life. They did not say anything, but neither one felt capable of capitulating so easily.

They found the Captain in the dining room, in a disheveled condition that did not accord with his habitual neatness: he was unshaven, his eyes were bloodshot from lack of sleep, his clothing was still sweaty from the previous night, his speech was interrupted by belches of anisette. Zenaida was asleep. They were beginning to eat their breakfast in silence, when a motor launch from the Health Department ordered them to stop the ship.

The Captain, standing on the bridge, shouted his answers to the questions put to him by the armed patrol. They wanted to know what kind of pestilence they carried on board, how many passengers there were, how many of them were sick, what possibility there was for new infections. The Captain replied that they had only three passengers on board and all of them had cholera, but they were being kept in strict seclusion. Those who were to come on board in La

Dorada, and the twenty-seven men of the crew, had not had any contact with them. But the commander of the patrol was not satisfied, and he ordered them to leave the bay and wait in Las Mercedes Marsh until two o'clock in the afternoon, while the forms were prepared for placing the ship in quarantine. The Captain let loose with a wagon driver's fart, and with a wave of his hand he ordered the pilot to turn around and go back to the marshes.

Fermina Daza and Florentino Ariza had heard everything from their table, but that did not seem to matter to the Captain. He continued to eat in silence, and his bad humor was evident in the manner in which he breached the rules of etiquette that sustained the legendary reputation of the riverboat captains. He broke apart his four fried eggs with the tip of his knife, and he ate them with slices of green plantain, which he placed whole in his mouth and chewed with savage delight. Fermina Daza and Florentino Ariza looked at him without speaking, as if waiting on a school bench to hear their final grades. They had not exchanged a word during his conversation with the health patrol, nor did they have the slightest idea of what would become of their lives, but they both knew that the Captain was thinking for them: they could see it in the throbbing of his temples.

While he finished off his portion of eggs, the tray of fried plantains, and the pot of *café con leche*, the ship left the bay with its boilers quiet, made its way along the channels through blankets of *taruya*, the river lotus with purple blossoms and large heart-shaped leaves, and returned to the marshes. The water was iridescent with the universe of fishes floating on their sides, killed by the dynamite of stealthy fishermen, and all the birds of the earth and the water circled above them with metallic cries. The wind from the Caribbean blew in the windows along with the racket made by the birds, and Fermina Daza felt in her blood the wild beating of her free will. To her right, the muddy, frugal estuary of the Great Magdalena River spread out to the other side of the world.

When there was nothing left to eat on the plates, the Captain wiped his lips with a corner of the tablecloth and broke into indecent slang that ended once and for all the reputation for fine speech enjoyed by the riverboat captains. For he was not speaking to them or to anyone else, but was trying instead to come to terms with his own rage. His conclusion, after a string of barbaric curses, was that he could find no way out of the mess he had gotten into with the cholera flag.

Florentino Ariza listened to him without blinking. Then he looked through the windows at the complete circle of the quadrant on the mariner's compass, the clear horizon, the December sky without a single cloud, the waters that could be navigated forever, and he said:

"Let us keep going, going, going, back to La Dorada."

Fermina Daza shuddered because she recognized his former voice, illuminated by the grace of the Holy Spirit, and she looked at the Captain: he was their destiny. But the Captain did not see her because he was stupefied by Florentino Ariza's tremendous powers of inspiration.

"Do you mean what you say?" he asked.

"From the moment I was born," said Florentino Ariza, "I have never said anything I did not mean."

The Captain looked at Fermina Daza and saw on her eyelashes the first glimmer of wintry frost. Then he looked at Florentino Ariza, his invincible power, his intrepid love, and he was overwhelmed by the belated suspicion that it is life, more than death, that has no limits.

"And how long do you think we can keep up this goddamn coming and going?" he asked.

Florentino Ariza had kept his answer ready for fifty-three years, seven months, and eleven days and nights.

"Forever," he said.

William Carlos Williams

The Ivy Crown

The whole process is a lie,
unless,
crowned by excess,
it break forcefully,
one way or another,
from its confinement—
or find a deeper well.
Antony and Cleopatra
were right;
they have shown

the way. I love you
or I do not live
at all.

Daffodil time
is past. This is
summer, summer!
the heart says,
and not even the full of it.
No doubts
are permitted—
though they will come
and may
before our time
overwhelm us.
We are only mortal
but being mortal
can defy our fate.
We may
by an outside chance
even win! We do not
look to see
jonquils and violets
come again

but there are,
still,
the roses!

Romance has no part in it.
The business of love is
cruelty *which*,
by our wills,
we transform
to live together.
It has its seasons,
for and against,
whatever the heart
fumbles in the dark
to assert
toward the end of May.
Just as the nature of briars
is to tear flesh,
I have proceeded
through them.
Keep
the briars out,
they say.

You cannot live
and keep free of
briars.

Children pick flowers.
Let them.
Though having them
in hand
they have no further use for them
but leave them crumpled
at the curb's edge.

At our age the imagination
across the sorry facts
lifts us
to make roses
stand before thorns.
Sure
love is cruel
and selfish
and totally obtuse—
at least, blinded by the light,

young love is.
But we are older,
I to love
and you to be loved,
we have,
no matter how,
by our wills survived
to keep
the jeweled prize
always
at our finger tips.
We will it so
and so it is
past all accident.

Notes on the Authors

ALICE ADAMS (b. 1926) is an American novelist and short story writer, living in California. "A Wonderful Woman" is from a collection of short stories published when she was fifty-six.

PAUL THE SILENTIARY (d. ca. 575) was a writer of epigrams and an usher (*silentarius*) at the court of the Byzantine emperor Justinian. Of his eighty-one poems preserved in that curious Byzantine compilation, *The Greek Anthology*, forty deal with the subject of love.

BERNARD SLADE (b. 1930), born in Canada, is a writer for stage, screen, and television. *Same Time, Next Year*, his most successful play, was first produced in New York City at the Brooks Atkinson Theatre in 1975.

PABLO NERUDA (1904–1973) won the Nobel Prize for Literature in 1971. *One Hundred Love Sonnets*, the collection from which the poem included here is taken, was published in 1960 and dedicated to the Chilean writer's third wife, Matilde Urrutia.

WILLIAM SHAKESPEARE (1564–1616) wrote the majority of his sonnets in the 1590s. We do not know to whom these poems were addressed.

ETHAN CANIN (b. 1960), a native of California, is the author of numerous short stories. "We Are Nighttime Travelers" was published in 1988, while he was attending medical school.

EDITH WHARTON (1862–1937), in addition to her many novels, short stories, and works of nonfiction, wrote more than four thousand letters in her lifetime. Some three hundred of these were sent to the journalist Morton Fullerton, with whom she had an intense extramarital affair between 1908 and 1910. Wharton was forty-six, a few years older than Fullerton, when their affair began. Her side of the correspondence reveals emotional awakening followed by self-abasement and despair.

RICHARD BAUSCH (b. 1945) is a novelist and short story writer who lives in Virginia. "Letter to the Lady of the House" appeared in the 1990 collection *The Fireman's Wife and Other Stories.*

PHILODEMUS (ca. 110–40 B.C.), born at Gadara in Palestine, was an Epicurean philosopher and poet. He had considerable influence on many educated Romans of his day.

WILLIAM BUTLER YEATS (1865–1939), Irish poet and playwright, was the 1923 Nobel laureate in literature. After a long and unsuccessful attempt to win the love of Maud Gonne, he married Georgie Hyde Lees, when he was in his early fifties.

EDMUND WILSON (1895–1972), a prolific American writer and critic, began keeping a journal when he was in his twenties. The section quoted here, dating from 1970, was written in Talcottville, New York, where the seventy-five-year-old Wilson was as usual spending the summer removed from his wife, Elena Thornton: she preferred to remain at their house on Cape Cod.

SAMUEL SEWALL (1652–1739) is perhaps best known as the hanging judge of the Salem witch trials; he later acknowledged the sentences he delivered as unjust. Originally a merchant in Boston, he became a judge of the Superior Court of Massachusetts and then chief justice. He was left a widower in 1717, after almost forty-two years of marriage to his first wife, and two years later he remarried. In 1720, several months after his second wife died, Sewall began his courtship of the widow Katherine Winthrop. He was sixty-eight, she fifty-six.

STEVIE SMITH (1902–1971), an English poet and novelist, maintained a certain distrust of romantic love. She remarked that "separateness is our nature, never can two be one, nobody would wish it."

MAYA ANGELOU (b. 1928) is an American novelist, poet, actress, and activist. "Many and More" comes from *I Shall Not Be Moved*, a book of poetry issued when Angelou was sixty-two.

MICHELANGELO BUONARROTI (1475–1564), known primarily as a sculptor, painter, and architect, was also a poet. He wrote a number of poems to the Marchesa Vittoria Colonna, a poet, between 1544 and her death (at fifty-seven) in 1547, when he was seventy-two.

ANTON CHEKHOV (1860–1904), the son of former serfs, was trained to be a doctor. Of his two careers he observed: "Medicine is my lawful wife and literature my mistress. When I get fed up with the one, I spend the night with the other. Though it is irregular, it is less boring this way." Writing was his chief source of income. Chekhov himself celebrated love in later life. He did not marry until age forty-one (his wife was the actress Olga Knipper), only three years before his death.

ARCHIBALD MACLEISH (1892–1982) was an American poet who received the 1953 Pulitzer Prize in Poetry for his *Collected Poems 1917–1952*.

EDNA O'BRIEN (b. 1932) is an Irish writer of novels, short stories, plays, screenplays, nonfiction, and children's fiction. "Mrs. Reinhardt" comes from *Mrs. Reinhardt and Other Stories*, published in 1978.

ADRIENNE RICH (b. 1929) is an American poet and feminist. Her poem in this anthology is from *Twenty-one Love Poems*, a series of verses written to a woman between 1974 and 1976.

MAY SARTON (b. 1912), who lives in Maine, is a poet, novelist, diarist, and autobiographer. "Old Lovers at the Ballet" is from her collection *Halfway to Silence*, which was issued in 1980.

GLENN BUSCH (b. 1948) is a writer and photographer from New Zealand. He is the author of *Working Men*, a book of interviews with and photographs of laborers, as well as *You Are My Darling Zita*, a book of interviews with elderly New Zealanders.

ELLEN GILCHRIST (b. 1935) is the author of many novels and short story collections. She lives in Fayetteville, Arkansas.

GABRIEL GARCÍA MÁRQUEZ (b. 1928) is a Colombian novelist and journalist who was awarded the Nobel Prize for Literature in 1982. His novel *Love in the Time of Cholera* was published in 1985.

WILLIAM CARLOS WILLIAMS (1883–1963) was, like Chekhov, a physician as well as a writer. "The Ivy Crown," published when this American poet was seventy-two, was part of the collection *Journey to Love*, which was dedicated to Williams's wife of more than forty years.

The publisher gratefully acknowledges permission to reprint material from the following sources. Where no credit is given, every effort was made to contact the copyright owner and secure permission.

Alice Adams, *To See You Again*. Copyright © 1982 by Alice Adams. Reprinted by permission of Alfred A. Knopf, Inc.

Bernard Slade, *Same Time, Next Year*. Copyright © 1975 by Bernard Slade. Reprinted by permission of Samuel French, Inc.

Pablo Neruda, *One Hundred Love Sonnets*, trans. Stephen Tapscott. Copyright © 1959 by Pablo Neruda. Copyright © 1986 by The Texas University Press. Reprinted by permission of The Texas University Press.

Ethan Canin, *Emperor of the Air*. Copyright © 1988 by Ethan Canin. Reprinted by permission of Houghton Mifflin Co. All rights reserved.

Edith Wharton, "Letter to W. Morton Fullerton, August 26, 1908," from The Harry Ransom Humanities Research Center at the University of Texas at Austin. Reprinted by permission of the Estate of Edith Wharton and Watkins/Loomis Agency.

Richard Bausch, *The Fireman's Wife and Other Stories*. Copyright © 1990 by Richard Bausch. Reprinted by permission of Simon & Schuster, Inc.

Philodemus, *Poems from the Greek Anthology*, trans. Kenneth Rexroth. Copyright © 1962 by The University of Michigan. Reprinted by permission of The University of Michigan Press.

William Butler Yeats, *The Poems of W. B. Yeats: A New Edition*, ed. Richard J. Finneran. Copyright © 1940 by Georgie Yeats. Copyright renewed © 1968 by Bertha Georgie Yeats, Michael Butler Yeats, and Anne Yeats. Reprinted by permission of the Macmillan Publishing Company.

Edmund Wilson, *The Sixties*. Copyright © 1993 by Helen Miranda Wilson. Reprinted by permission of Farrar, Straus & Giroux, Inc.

Samuel Sewall, *The Diary of Samuel Sewall 1674–1729*, ed. Halsey Thomas. Copyright © 1973 by Farrar, Straus & Giroux, Inc. Reprinted by permission of Farrar, Straus & Giroux, Inc.

Stevie Smith, *Collected Poems of Stevie Smith*. Copyright © 1972 by Stevie Smith. Reprinted by permission of New Directions Publishing Corp.

Maya Angelou, *I Shall Not Be Moved*. Copyright © 1990 by Maya Angelou. Reprinted by permission of Random House, Inc.

Michelangelo Buonarroti, *The Complete Poetry of Michelangelo*, trans. Sidney Alexander. Copyright © 1991 by Sidney Alexander. Reprinted by permission of The Ohio University Press/Swallow Press, Athens.

Anton Chekhov, *The Portable Chekhov*, trans. and ed. Avrahm Yarmolinsky. Copyright © 1947, 1968 by Viking Penguin, Inc. Copyright © renewed 1975 by Avrahm Yarmolinsky. Reprinted by permission of Viking Penguin, a division of Penguin Books USA Inc.

Archibald MacLeish, *Collected Poems 1917–1982*. Copyright © 1985 by the Estate of Archibald MacLeish. Reprinted by permission of Houghton Mifflin Co. All rights reserved.

Edna O'Brien, "Mrs. Reinhardt" from *A Fanatic Heart*. Copyright © 1984 by Edna O'Brien. Reprinted by permission of Farrar, Straus & Giroux, Inc.

Adrienne Rich, "Twenty-one Love Poems" from *The Dream of a Common Language, Poems 1974–1977*. Copyright © 1978 W. W. Norton & Company, Inc. Reprinted by permission of the author and W. W. Norton & Company, Inc.

May Sarton, *Halfway to Silence*. Copyright © 1980 by May Sarton. Reprinted by permission of W. W. Norton & Company, Inc.

Glenn Busch, *You Are My Darling Zita*. Copyright © 1991 by Glenn Busch. Reprinted by permission of Temple University Press.

Ellen Gilchrist, *Drunk with Love*. Copyright © 1986 by Ellen Gilchrist. Reprinted by permission of Little, Brown and Company.

Gabriel García Márquez, *Love in the Time of Cholera*, trans. E. Grossman. Copyright © 1985 by Gabriel García Márquez. Copyright © 1988 by Alfred A. Knopf, Inc. Reprinted by permission of Alfred A. Knopf, Inc.

William Carlos Williams, *The Collected Poems of William Carlos Williams 1939–1962*, vol. 2. Copyright © 1944, 1948, 1962 by William Carlos Williams. Reprinted by permission of New Directions Publishing Corp.